Fioretti:
The Little Flowers
of Pope Francis

ANDREA TORNIELLI

Fioretti: The Little Flowers of Pope Francis

~

Heartwarming Stories of the Gospel in Action

Translated by William J. Melcher

IGNATIUS PRESS   SAN FRANCISCO

Original Italian edition:
I fioretti di Papa Francesco
© 2013 Edizioni Piemme Spa, Milan
www.edizpiemme.it

Unless otherwise indicated, citations from papal
documents, homilies, and interviews are largely
taken from the Vatican website or www.news.va

Cover design by John Herreid

In memory of Nora and Nando,
who are watching us from above

Contents

Little Flowers of Everyday Holiness

Little Flowers on the Telephone

Marian Little Flowers

Little Flowers with a Smile

Little Flowers of Courage

Little Flowers of Sharing

Introduction

The Fragrance of the Gospel

Since the evening of March 13, 2013, when the conclave elected a Pope who had come "from the end of the earth", the gestures, words, and witness of Francis have impressed and continue to move a great many people in the world.

It is worthwhile returning for a moment to the memory of that March evening, when the new Pope, appearing on the central balcony of St. Peter's, had the whole square pray, reciting the Our Father, Hail Mary, and Glory be, and before blessing the men and women of his new diocese and of the entire world, asked the crowd, the people of God, to pray for him.

The election, which took place very rapidly, as had been the case with the election of his predecessor, was a surprise. Just as the announcement, one month before, of the resignation by Benedict XVI had been a surprise.

Two basic things stand out, which help to explain the attention and the sympathy prompted by Francis, even in distant circles. This sympathetic attention gives no sign of diminishing, despite predictions about the end of the media "honeymoon" that have been made by those who seem sometimes to regret the recent experiences of the Church "under attack".

The first is his personal witness to the Gospel message: little gestures and big ones, the minor or major choices that he has made each day, his ability to meet everyone and to speak to everyone, his simple way of being himself, have made him not only credible but above all close. The Pope is perceived by many, many people throughout the world as "one of us". It is enough to watch him embrace the sick, the suffering, children. It is enough to see how much time he spends among the people before and after his Wednesday audiences, to notice this closeness of the Bishop of Rome who is not afraid of tenderness. "We must not be afraid of tenderness!" he repeated from the first acts of his new ministry as Bishop of Rome. Moreover the changes that he has brought about are there for everyone to see, in keeping with the unprecedented name that the Jesuit Pope chose to take: the name of the *Poverello*, the Little Poor Man of Assisi.

The second thing is the magisterium consisting of the homilies at the Mass that he celebrates each day in the Domus Sanctae Marthae. Short commentaries on the readings of the day, an encounter that is expected every morning. A "bit-by-bit catechesis" (*Catechetica in briciole* was the title of a book by Albino Luciani [Pope John Paul I], who cared very much about the simplicity of preaching) which is at the same time profound and capable of touching the hearts of individuals. Day after day, this magisterium is guiding many believers, many more than major encyclicals or important cultural debates could ever reach.

The message that Francis considers most important, as he himself said in his homily at the Mass in the Vatican parish of St. Anna on March 17, is the message of mercy. "Without mercy", he said to the Brazilian bishops during his journey to Rio de Janeiro, "we have little chance nowadays of becoming part of a world of 'wounded' persons in need of understanding, forgiveness, love." He added, "We need a church able to make sense of the 'night' contained in the flight of so many of our brothers and sisters. . . . We need a church unafraid of going forth into their night . . . a church capable of meeting them on their way."

"I dream of a church that is a mother and shepherdess", Francis said during his interview with the editor of *La Civiltà Cattolica*, Antonio Spadaro [which was published in English by *America*]. "The church's ministers must be merciful, take responsibility for the people and accompany them like the good Samaritan, who washes, cleans, and raises up his neighbor. This is pure Gospel. God is greater than sin."

The Pope added:

> The structural and organizational reforms are secondary —that is, they come afterward. The first reform must be the attitude. The ministers of the Gospel must be people who can warm the hearts of the people, who walk through the dark night with them, who know how to dialogue and to descend themselves into their people's night, into the darkness, but without getting lost. The people of God want pastors, not clergy acting like bureaucrats or government officials. The bishops, particularly, must be able to support the movements of God among their people with patience, so that no one is left behind. But they must also be able

to accompany the flock that has a flair for finding new paths. Instead of being just a church that welcomes and receives by keeping the doors open, let us try also to be a church that finds new roads, that is able to step outside itself and go to those who do not attend Mass, to those who have quit or are indifferent. The ones who quit sometimes do it for reasons that, if properly understood and assessed, can lead to a return. But that takes audacity and courage.

One fact that is obvious to anyone who is trying to look at reality—and does not allow himself to be affected by nostalgic prejudices, by his own tastes in ecclesiastical attire, or else by the self-referential debate of some intellectual circles that often flattened the profound Magisterium of Pope Benedict XVI into the dimensions of an exclusively law-and-order Church—is that the pontificate of Francis has given many people a second wind.

Francis' attitude of "humility and closeness", this return to the essentials of the Christian faith and to the radical character of the Gospel, is the distinctive sign of this initial period. A closeness capable of "warming hearts", which was manifested in full force on the occasion of his first journey outside of Rome, in July 2013, when the Pope traveled to Lampedusa to visit the immigrants who land there on the old, unsafe boats that too often turn into coffins sunk in the depths of the sea.

A closeness that emerged during the journey to Brazil, which culminated with a visit of the Pontiff to a *favela* [slum].

"If we step outside ourselves", Francis said during the Vigil of Pentecost with the ecclesial movements, "we find poverty."

> Today—it sickens the heart to say so—the discovery of a tramp who has died of the cold is not news. . . . Today, the thought that a great many children do not have food to eat is not news. This is serious, this is serious! We cannot put up with this! . . . We cannot become starched Christians, those over-educated Christians who speak of theological matters as they calmly sip their tea. No! We must become courageous Christians and go in search of the people who are the very flesh of Christ!

This book contains incidents, excerpts from homilies, testimonies, encounters, telephone calls that have Pope Francis as their protagonist. The title echoes the *Little Flowers of St. Francis*, the famous collection of stories about the beloved Francis of Assisi, whose name the Pope adopted for himself. The present work makes no claim to completeness, nor does it intend to offer a systematic account of the first months of Francis' pontificate or to present analyses and commentaries. It merely tries to offer a collection of fragments, a little selection which, page after page, may help the reader to become better acquainted with the Bishop of Rome who came "from the end of the earth".

~

LITTLE FLOWERS
OF MERCY

~

Infinite Mercy

People today certainly need words, but most of all they need us to bear witness to the mercy and tenderness of the Lord.

*Homily during a Mass for
seminarians and novices, July 7, 2013*

T he new Pope celebrated his first Mass with the faithful in the little parish church of St. Anna, in the Vatican, on Sunday, March 17. Francis gave the homily, speaking off the cuff. "Jesus has this message for us: mercy. I think—and I say it with humility—that this is the Lord's most powerful message."

The Pope commented on the Gospel passage about the adulterous woman, whom the scribes and Pharisees were about to stone, as prescribed by the Mosaic law. Jesus saved her life by demanding that someone who was without sin should cast the first stone: and they all went away. "Neither do I condemn you; go, and do not sin again", Jesus had said to the woman. Bergoglio, referring to the scribes and Pharisees who had dragged the woman they were going to stone into the Nazarene's presence, said: "We too, . . . at times, like to find a stick to beat others with, to condemn others."

The first and only step required in order to experience God's infinite mercy, Francis explained, is to acknowledge one's need of his forgiveness: "Jesus . . . comes for us, when we recognize that we are sinners." It is enough to avoid imitating the Pharisee who stood before the altar and thanked God that he was "not like other men". If we are like that Pharisee, if we think that we are just, "then we do not know the Lord's heart, and we will never have the joy of experiencing this mercy!"

Someone who habitually judges others, feels that he is okay, and considers himself just and good, does not notice that he needs to be embraced and forgiven. But there are also those who do notice that need but think that they can not be redeemed because they have committed too much evil.

The Pope, who even as a bishop had the habit of spending time in the confessional, related in this connection a conversation with a man who, upon hearing these words about mercy, had replied to Bergoglio as follows: "Oh, Father, if you knew my life, you would not say that to me! I am a great sinner!" He answered:

> All the better! Go to Jesus: he likes you to tell him these things! He forgets, he has a very special capacity for forgetting. He forgets, he kisses you, he embraces you and he simply says to you: "Neither do I condemn you; go, and sin no more." That is the only advice he gives you. After a month, if we are in the same situation. . . . Let us go back to the Lord. The Lord never tires of forgiving: never! It is we who tire of asking his forgiveness. Let us ask for the grace not to tire of asking forgiveness, because he never tires of forgiving.

God never tires of welcoming and pardoning, if only we acknowledge that we need his forgiveness. These simple, profound words of Francis are a breath of oxygen. For so many people. Precisely because they present the face of a Church that does not reproach people for their fragility and their wounds, but treats them with the medicine of mercy. A Church that embraces.

The Pope added, referring to the Gospel about the adulterous woman: "Jesus' attitude is striking. . . . We do not hear words of condemnation but only words of love." It is so easy for us to become indignant about the sins of others, to ask for condemnations without making an examination of conscience. "The face of God is the face of a merciful Father who always has patience", Francis says. "He does not tire of forgiving us if we are able to return to him with a contrite heart", he adds. And to acknowledge that we need to be forgiven.

Shortly after this homily, given in the church of St. Anna, Francis appeared at the window of the study of the Apostolic Palace for his first Angelus. "Mercy . . . changes the world. A little mercy makes the world less cold and more just", he said, citing the prophet Isaiah: "Even if our sins were scarlet, God's love would make them white as snow." To a world that has such trouble believing, the new Pope wants to shout the same proclamation of two thousand years ago, namely, that this mercy is not a feeling but a person. His remarkable way of recalling the Incarnation—the Angelus is precisely the memorial of the Incarnation—is a maternal gesture: he holds his arms in front of him and moves them as though rocking a baby and says: "Our

Lady . . . held in her arms the Mercy of God made man,
Jesus."

Then another anecdote, another personal recollection
from his long, daily experience as a confessor. Francis tells
about an old woman who had confessed to him when he
was an auxiliary bishop in Buenos Aires, during an out-
door Mass in the presence of the Pilgrim Virgin Statue of
Our Lady of Fatima. "She said to me: 'We all have sins,
but the Lord forgives all things.' And I said: 'But how
do you know, Madam?' She answered: 'If the Lord did
not forgive everything, the world would not exist.'"
Bergoglio's reply was: "Tell me, Madam, did you study at
the Gregorian [University]?" That old woman without
any diplomas or degrees from pontifical universities had
marvelously and very effectively expressed a great truth
of the faith.

We live in a society where we become less and less accustomed to acknowledging our responsibilities and blaming
ourselves for our mistakes: indeed, it is always someone
else's fault. Other people are always the immoral ones;
someone else is always at fault, never me. We also experience a certain view of the Church that sees her only im-
posing requirements and prohibitions that stifle freedom
and weigh down everyday life, which is already burden-
some. The message of mercy knocks down both clichés
at the same time.

There is no doubt that these words of the Pope made
an impression on the hearts of many people. Above all
on the fallen-away, on those who have distanced them-

selves from the Church and from the practice of their faith. Many pastors from all parts of Italy have testified to this, speaking about the increase in the number of confessions in the Easter season and about the fact that many penitents specifically cited Francis' words about mercy.

The sociologist Massimo Introvigne, director of CESNUR (*Centro Studi sulle Nuove Religioni* [Center for Studies on the New Religions]), conducted a survey on the "Francis effect". In other words, on returns to the Church and to the Sacraments on the part of individuals who had fallen away and were struck by the words of Pope Bergoglio about mercy and forgiveness.

"From anecdotal evidence", Introvigne explained, "we tried to make a transition to scientific observation, however initial and preliminary it may be. We distributed a questionnaire by means of so-called cascade technology that utilizes the social networks Facebook and Twitter, starting with groups that are visited particularly by Catholics."

"Assuming", the sociologist continued, "that, as with all technologies, this one too has its advantages and limitations with regard to sampling, and that the effects connected with the first period of a new pontificate must always be verified at a distance of several months so as to ascertain whether they are ephemeral or lasting, out of a sample of two hundred priests and religious, 53 percent stated that they had encountered in their own community an increase of persons who are returning to the Church or going to confession, adding that these persons explicitly cite the appeals of Pope Francis as the reason for their return to religious practice."

"In 43.8 percent of these cases, the increase in the number of faithful is described as consistent, greater than 25 percent. Religious priests (66.7%) note this more often in comparison to diocesan priests (50%). And for 64.2 percent of the sample the increase pertains to confessions in particular. We conducted the same survey", Introvigne continues, "on a sample of more than five hundred Catholic lay people. They perceive the Francis effect less than the priests and religious, but are directly involved in the confessions. But a significant 41.8 percent of the laity have noticed the effect, which therefore seems to be visible to the naked eye, so to speak."

"These findings", the sociologist concludes, "are very significant, within the limits of the survey. An effect observed by more than half of a sample is a phenomenon that not only exists but is of great importance. If we were to seek to translate the data into numerical terms on a national scale, with reference to half of the parishes and communities, we would have to speak about hundreds of thousands of persons who are returning to the Church, accepting the invitations of Pope Francis."

～

"My Church, a field hospital"

Although the life of a person is a land full of thorns and weeds, there is always a space in which the good seed can grow. You have to trust God.

Interview with La Civiltà Cattolica, *September 19, 2013*

What does the Church need today? Pope Francis explained it in the interview with Fr. Antonio Spadaro, editor of *La Civiltà Cattolica*. And he used a suggestive image, that of a field hospital after a battle.

I see clearly that the thing the Church needs most today is the ability to heal wounds and to warm the hearts of the faithful; it needs nearness, proximity. I see the Church as a field hospital after battle. It is useless to ask a seriously injured person if he has high cholesterol and about the level of his blood sugars! You have to heal his wounds. Then we can talk about everything else. Heal the wounds, heal the wounds. . . . And you have to start from the ground up.

As if to say: someone who has lost his way in life, who is living in a very unusual, "irregular", or desperate situation, needs first of all to encounter the face of mercy, not to be confronted with a list of rules and precepts, or a series of tests on his own sins.

Francis continued:

> The Church sometimes has locked itself up in small things, in small-minded rules. The most important thing is the first proclamation: Jesus Christ has saved you. And the ministers of the Church must be ministers of mercy above all. The confessor, for example, is always in danger of being either too much of a rigorist or too lax. Neither is merciful, because neither of them really takes responsibility for the person. The rigorist washes his hands so that he leaves it to the commandment. The loose minister washes his hands by simply saying, "This is not a sin" or something like that. In pastoral ministry we must accompany people, and we must heal their wounds.

"How are we treating the people of God?" He continued, revealing a dream of his:

> I dream of a Church that is a mother and shepherdess. The Church's ministers must be merciful, take responsibility for the people and accompany them like the good Samaritan, who washes, cleans, and raises up his neighbor. This is pure Gospel. God is greater than sin. The structural and organizational reforms are secondary —that is, they come afterward. The first reform must be the attitude. The ministers of the Gospel must be people who can warm the hearts of the people, who walk through the dark night with them, who know how to dialogue and to descend themselves into their people's night, into the darkness, but without getting

lost. The people of God want pastors, not clergy acting like bureaucrats or government officials. The bishops, particularly, must be able to support the movements of God among their people with patience, so that no one is left behind. But they must also be able to accompany the flock that has a flair for finding new paths.

The Gift of Tears

We are all jars of clay, fragile and poor, yet we carry within us an immense treasure.

@Pontifex (Pope Francis on Twitter),
August 9, 2013

On the day when the Church celebrates the feast of the Exaltation of the Holy Cross, Pope Francis, preaching in the chapel of the Domus Sanctae Marthae, spoke about this mystery and declared that it can be understood only by someone on his knees and in tears, and never alone. The Pope explained—as Vatican Radio reported—that in the mystery of the Cross we discover the history of man and the history of God, summarized by the Fathers of the Church in the comparison between the tree of the knowledge of good and evil, in Eden, and the tree of the Cross.

Referring to the former, Francis said: "That tree did such great harm", whereas the tree of the Cross "brings us salvation and health, and pardons that harm". It is this "itinerary that human history follows". It is a way that enables us "to encounter Jesus Christ the Redeemer, who

---

To read Pope Francis' @Pontifex posts, see http://twitter.com/pontifex

lays down his life for love". Indeed, God did not send his Son into the world to condemn the world, but so that the world might be saved by him.

"This tree of the cross", he added, "saves us all from the consequences of that other tree, where self-sufficiency began along with pride and the arrogance to want to know everything, according to our mentality, according to our criteria, and also according to the presumption that we are and become the sole judges of the world. This is man's history: from one tree to the other."

Francis then stated that in the Cross we find also "the history of God", because God "wanted to take on our history and to walk beside us", by becoming a servant and dying on Calvary:

God took this itinerary out of love, there is no other explanation: only love does such things. Today we look at the cross, the history of man and the history of God. We look at this cross, where we can try a taste of that aloe honey, that bitter sweetness of Jesus' sacrifice. But this mystery is so great, and by ourselves we cannot look correctly at this mystery, not so much to understand—yes, to understand . . .—but rather to sense profoundly the salvation of this mystery. First of all the mystery of the cross. It can be understood only on our knees, in prayer, but also in the midst of tears: tears are what bring us close to this mystery.

The Pope emphasized:

Without shedding tears, heartfelt tears, we shall never understand this mystery. It is the weeping of the penitent, the weeping of our brother and sister who see so many human miseries and likewise see them in Jesus, on his knees weeping . . . and never alone, never alone!

"In order to enter into this mystery," Francis concluded, "which is not a labyrinth but resembles us a bit, we always need our mother, our Mamma's hand. May she, Mary, make us sense how great and how humble this mystery is; how sweet as honey and how bitter as aloe. May she be the one to accompany us along this path, which no one else can take if not we ourselves. Everyone must follow it. With our Mamma, weeping and on our knees."

∼

The Confessional
"is not a dry-cleaner's shop"

I want a Church that is close to the people.

Interview during his journey to
Rio de Janeiro, July 25, 2013

The confessional is not a "dry cleaning establishment" that cleanses us from sins, nor a "torture chamber" where the unfortunate penitent is beaten with a club. Rather, it is an encounter with Jesus, an encounter with his tenderness. But it is necessary to go to confession without lies or half-truths, with meekness and gladness, confident and armed with that "blessed shame" that is "the virtue of the humble". The virtue of acknowledging that we are sinners, in need of God's infinite mercy.

This is the message proclaimed by Francis during his homily at the morning Mass he celebrated in the chapel of the Domus Sanctae Marthae on April 29, 2013.

The Pope began with a reflection on the First Letter of John, in which the Apostle speaks to the first Christians and he does so with simplicity: "God is light and in him is no darkness at all." But "if we say we have fellowship with him", that we are friends of the Lord, "while we walk in darkness, we lie and do not live according to the truth." We must adore God in spirit and in truth.

"What does it mean", Bergoglio asked, "to walk in darkness? Because all of us have some darkness in our life, and also moments when everything is darkness, even in our own conscience, do we not? To walk in darkness means to be satisfied with oneself. To be convinced that one does not need salvation. This is darkness!"

Francis continued:

> When someone walks along this path of darkness, it is not easy to turn back. Therefore, John continues, per-haps this way of thinking made him reflect: "If we say we have no sin, we deceive ourselves, and the truth is not in us." Look at your sins, at our sins: we are all sin-ners, all of us. This is the point of departure. But "if we confess our sins, he is faithful and just, and will for-give our sins and cleanse us from all unrighteousness." And he presents to us, does he not, this Lord who is so good, so faithful, so just, who forgives us. When the Lord forgives us, he does justice. Yes, he does justice first to himself, because he came to save and when he pardons us he does justice to himself. "I am your sal-vation", and he welcomes us.

This welcome characterizes the spirit of Psalm 103[102]: " 'As a father pities his children, so the LORD pities those who fear him', those who go to him. The tenderness of the Lord. He always understands us, but also he does not let us talk: He knows everything. 'Be quiet, go in peace', the peace that he alone gives."

This is what "happens in the sacrament of reconciliation. Many times", Francis added, "we think that going to confession is like going to a dry-cleaning establishment. But Jesus in the confessional is not a torture chamber." Confession is "an encounter with Jesus who waits for us as we are."

> "But listen, Lord, I am like this." It embarrasses us to tell the truth: I did this, I thought that. But shame is a true Christian virtue and also a human virtue. The ability to be ashamed: I do not know whether people say this in Italian, but in our country they say that those who are incapable of shame are *sin vergüenza*. That person "has no shame" because he does not have the ability to be ashamed. And to be ashamed is a virtue of the humble person.

Bergoglio then commented on the passage from the Letter of St. John. These are words, he said, that invite us to have confidence:

> The Paraclete is at our side and supports us in the Father's presence. He sustains our weak life, our sin. He forgives us. He is precisely our defender, because he supports us. Now, how should we go to the Lord, in this way, with our truth as sinners? With confidence, even with gladness, without disguising ourselves. We must never disguise ourselves before God! With truth. In shame? Blessed shame, that is a virtue.

Jesus therefore waits for each one of us, Francis explained, citing the Gospel of Matthew:

> "Come to me, all who labor and are heavy laden", even by sin, "and I will give you rest. Take my yoke upon

you, and learn from me; for I am gentle and lowly in heart." This is the virtue that Jesus asks of us: humility and meekness.

Humility and meekness are like the frame around a Christian life. A Christian always walks that way, in humility and meekness. And Jesus waits for us so as to forgive us. We can make a request of him: then going to confession is not going to a torture chamber? No! It is going to praise God, because I, a sinner, have been saved by him. And is he waiting for me to beat me? No, with tenderness to forgive you. What if I do the same thing tomorrow? Go once again, and go and go and go. He always waits for you. This tenderness of the Lord, this humility, this meekness.

Francis concluded his homily by inviting the faithful to have confidence in John's words: "If any one does sin, we have an advocate with the Father." And he declared: "This is encouraging. Beautiful, isn't it? And if we are ashamed? Blessed shame, because that is a virtue. The Lord gives us this grace, this courage always to go to him with the truth, because the truth is light. And not with the darkness of half-truths or lies in the presence of God."

∿

When Gossip Kills

The only way for the life of peoples to progress, is via the culture of encounter, a culture in which all have something good to give and all can receive something good in return.

Address at the Municipal Theater,
Rio de Janeiro, July 27, 2013

There are slanderers and gossips who "kill". Pope Francis is convinced of this and several times, in his homilies during Mass at the Domus Sanctae Marthae, he has spoken about it. Commenting on the Gospel that quotes Jesus' question, "Why do you see the speck that is in your brother's eye, but do not notice the log that is in your own?" on September 13, 2013, Bergoglio went on to speak about those who "judge their neighbor". A warning addressed to everyone, which brings everybody into the discussion, deftly portraying attitudes from which ecclesial and Vatican circles are not immune.

Jesus, the Pope said in the homily reported by Vatican Radio, after speaking to us about humility, speaks to us about its opposite, about that "hateful attitude to one's neighbor", about judging one's brother. And he does so using a "strong word: hypocrite".

[They live their lives] judging their neighbor, speaking evil of their neighbor. They are hypocrites because they don't have the strength, the courage to look at their own defects. The Lord doesn't say too much about this. Then, later he was to say: he who has hatred in his heart for his brother is a murderer. . . . The Apostle John says this very clearly in his First Letter: whoever hates his brother walks in darkness. Whoever judges his brother, walks in darkness.

Therefore, when "we judge our brothers in our hearts, or worse, when we speak badly of them with others, we are Christian murderers." "A Christian murderer. . . . I am not the one who says this, eh? The Lord says it", the Pope continued. "And on this point there is no room for nuances. If you speak ill of your brother, you kill your brother. And we, every time we do that, imitate the act of Cain, the first murderer in history."

Francis added that at a time when there is talk about wars and calls for peace, "some act of our own conversion is necessary." And this conversion concerns the habit of gossip also. "Slander", the Pope said, "always moves in the direction of crime. There is no such thing as innocent slander." We use the tongue, which ought to praise God, he continued, "to speak ill of our brother or sister, we use it to kill God . . . the image of God in our brother."

Francis then remarked: someone might say that a person deserved slander. If so, "Go pray for him! Go do penance for him!"

And then, if necessary, talk to that person who can remedy the problem. But do not tell everyone about it!

Paul was a great sinner, and he says about himself: "I formerly blasphemed and persecuted and insulted [the Lord]; but I received mercy." Maybe none of us blasphemes—maybe. But if one of us slanders, certainly he is an insulting persecutor. Let us beg for him, for the whole Church, the grace of conversion from the criminality of slander to love, humility, meekness, gentleness, and the magnanimity of love of neighbor.

∼

Suppose the Pope Recalls the Existence of the Devil

God desires mercy more than sacrifice.

Angelus in Albano, July 14, 2013

W hen we do not profess Jesus Christ, we profess the worldliness of the devil." So said Pope Francis in the homily of his first Mass as Pontiff, which he celebrated in the Sistine Chapel on the day after his election. The new Bishop of Rome, who had come "from the end of the earth", has mentioned the devil several times in his preaching. On St. Peter's Square on March 24, 2013, while celebrating World Youth Day, he recalled that the Christian's joy results not from possessing many things but from the encounter with Jesus, "from knowing that with him we are never alone, even at difficult moments, even when our life's journey comes up against problems and obstacles that seem insurmountable, and there are so many of them! And in this moment the enemy, the devil, comes." Whereas on May 4, during the morning Mass in the Domus Sanctae Marthae, reflecting on the persecution of Christians, Francis spoke about "the hate of the prince of the world for those who have been saved and redeemed by Jesus."

These repeated remarks prompted a reflection by Fr. Giandomenico Mucci in the pages of *La Civiltà Cattolica*. He wrote: "For several decades, Catholic preaching has forgotten about the devil, who is fully present in the documents of Vatican II itself. Some theologians have welcomed the opinion that Satan is the product of the human imagination, a figure dreamt up in pagan areas, which later penetrated into Jewish thought." This would explain "the stir which was created, among believers and non-believers alike, when the Pope preached about the devil."

Forgetting the devil is a phenomenon that has been particularly characteristic of the last fifty years. A Pope Bergoglio often cited in his teaching as a bishop, Paul VI, decided in 1975 to publish a study by the Congregation for the Doctrine of the Faith entitled "Christian faith and demonology", which countered the attempt to "demythologize the centuries-old doctrine of the Church on Satan." Three years earlier Pope Montini had devoted to this subject the catechesis at a General Audience, declaring that "one of the greatest needs of the Church today is to defend against the evil which we call the devil." Paul VI stressed that "evil is not simply the lack of something but rather something present and active, a living being who is spiritual, perverse and perverting. He is a horrifying, mysterious, and fearsome reality. Anyone who refuses to recognize his existence goes outside the framework of biblical and Church teaching."

These quotations of Francis should therefore be interpreted in the wake of the remarks by his predecessors, even though the Argentine Pope seems to be less hesitant to speak explicitly about the devil. He does so, however,

without indulging in that sensationalism that leads people to believe that the devil exists and manifests himself
only in extraordinary, spectacular events, such as cases of
diabolical possession or obsession: phenomena that might
give the impression that the devil exists only there and
does not act and work discreetly, on the other hand, in
the everyday life of each human being.

In this connection, a great commotion was caused by a
video of a prayer recited by Francis over a man seated in a
wheelchair at the edge of the crowd during a Wednesday
audience. The man appeared to be visibly disturbed and
the Pope placed his hands on his head. Newspaper and
television reports spoke about an exorcism, even though
the term was used improperly, since the rite of exorcism
is much more complex. The Press Office of the Holy See
explained that it was only a prayer and nothing more. But
the interested party, forty-three-year-old Angel V., who
is of Mexican descent and has two children, related after
the encounter on St. Peter's Square that he had been tormented by evil spirits since 1999. A case of possession
that a dozen different priest-exorcists had not been able
to alleviate at all. And he assured the interviewer that he
was better after that prayer recited over him by the Pontiff.

The discretion and reticence of the Vatican is under-
standable, however.

The conclusion of Fr. Mucci's article in *La Civiltà Cattolica* is interesting:

> There is a risk that Christians will attribute too much
> importance to the devil, seduced by the trash that can
> be seen in some newspapers or on some television chan-
> nels, which lead them to take pleasure in the unwhole-

some thrills brought about by interventions of the devil, whether real, presumed or made up. Satan exists and, with God's permission, tempts man toward evil and can cause him serious harm. But he cannot obstruct in us the life of the Gospel or eternal salvation. The devil is like a growling, ferocious dog, tethered to the wall with a strong chain. It can attack and kill only if someone comes close to the area within which the chain allows the beast to act. That chain is Christ.

~

"We will all see each other again in Purgatory"

Jesus is the door that leads to salvation, and is an open door to everyone.

@Pontifex (on Twitter), August 27, 2013

On Saturday, September 7, Pope Francis presided at the long vigil of prayer and adoration to beg for peace in Syria and in the world. It was the concluding event of a day entirely dedicated—by the Pontiff's decision—to fasting and prayer. The vigil lasted four hours and was marked by long intervals of silence.

That morning the Pope had an unscheduled meeting with around fifty pilgrims from Verona in the vicinity of the gate of the Holy Office; they had accompanied their pastor, who was there to donate an automobile, but only a few of them had been allowed to enter the Vatican. When he heard that, Francis decided to go and greet them. He borrowed a microphone from Tg5, an Italian television channel, and addressed a few words to them: "Today is a beautiful day because we must pray so much for peace, we must pray the Rosary", he said. "Now let me go", he added, "because I have to greet the others. Evidently you do not have your passports in order", he said, turning slightly toward the Vatican policemen responsible for his security, joking about the fact that those pilgrims had remained at the gate.

After that, Francis imparted his blessing. Then, shaking hands with the persons in front of him, he added: "See you soon. . . . And if not here, we will all meet again in Purgatory."

⌒

"Who am I? A sinner . . ."

Sin, even for those who do not have faith, exists
when one goes against one's conscience.

Letter to Eugenio Scalfari, La Repubblica,
September 11, 2013

"Who is Jorge Mario Bergoglio?" This is the question
that Fr. Antonio Spadaro asked the Pope during
the long interview published by *America* magazine. Francis stared at him in silence, made a sign that he accepted
the question and answered as follows: "I do not know
what might be the most fitting description. . . . I am a
sinner. This is the most accurate definition. It is not a figure of speech, a literary genre. I am a sinner." He added:

> Yes, perhaps I can say that I am a bit astute, that I can
> adapt to circumstances, but it is also true that I am a bit
> naïve. Yes, but the best summary, the one that comes
> more from the inside and I feel most true is this: I am
> a sinner whom the Lord has looked upon.

And he repeated: "I am one who is looked upon by the
Lord. I always felt my motto, *Miserando atque eligendo* [By

having mercy and by choosing him], was very true for
me."

Pope Francis' motto is taken from the *Homilies* of St.
Bede the Venerable, who in commenting on the Gospel
passage about the call of St. Matthew, writes: "Jesus saw
a publican and, since he looked upon him with feelings
of love and chose him, he said to him: 'Follow me.'"

Francis added: "I think the Latin gerund *miserando* is
impossible to translate in both Italian and Spanish. I like
to translate it with another gerund that does not exist:
misericordiando ['mercy-ing']."

Then the Pope continued to reflect on the basis of his
experience as a visitor to the Eternal City:

> I do not know Rome well. I know a few things. These
> include the Basilica of St. Mary Major; I always used
> to go there. I know St. Mary Major, St. Peter's . . .
> but when I had to come to Rome, I always stayed in
> [the neighborhood of] Via della Scrofa. From there I
> often visited the church of St. Louis of France, and I
> went there to contemplate the painting of *The Calling
> of St. Matthew* by Caravaggio.

"That finger of Jesus, pointing at Matthew. That's me.
I feel like him. Like Matthew." Here the interviewer, Fr.
Spadaro, notes that the Pope became determined, as if he
had found the image he was looking for:

> It is the gesture of Matthew that strikes me: he holds
> on to his money as if to say, "No, not me! No, this
> money is mine." Here, this is me, a sinner on whom

the Lord has turned his gaze. And this is what I said when they asked me if I would accept my election as pontiff.

～

God Is Greater than Any Sin

But make sure that [your mercy] is not sentiment, it is not being a "do-gooder"! On the contrary, mercy is the true force that can save man and the world from the "cancer" that is sin.

Angelus, September 15, 2013

Pope Francis is asking the whole Church for a pastoral conversion. He wants the bishops and priests, as well as all Christians, to be able to show the face of mercy, the proclamation of a God who is close and loving, capable of accepting and forgiving. "We cannot insist only on issues related to abortion, gay marriage, and the use of contraceptive methods. This is not possible", he said in the interview that he granted to the editor of *La Civiltà Cattolica*, Fr. Antonio Spadaro, and was published in English in *America* magazine.

"I have not spoken much about these things", Francis admitted, "and I was reprimanded for that. But when we speak about these issues, we have to talk about them in a context. The teaching of the Church, for that matter, is clear and I am a son of the Church, but it is not necessary to talk about these issues all the time."

The Pope also said:

> The Church's pastoral ministry cannot be obsessed with
> the transmission of a disjointed multitude of doctrines
> to be imposed insistently. Proclamation in a mission-
> ary style focuses on the essentials, on the necessary
> things: this is also what fascinates and attracts more,
> what makes the heart burn, as it did for the disciples
> at Emmaus. . . .

This is the essential thing. To see and hear Francis, to follow him as he meets people, the sick and the suffering,
makes one understand what it is about. "The Church
sometimes has locked itself up in small things, in small-
minded rules. The most important thing is the first proclamation: Jesus Christ has saved you. And the ministers of
the Church must be ministers of mercy above all. . . .
The proclamation of the saving love of God comes before moral and religious imperatives. Today sometimes it
seems that the opposite order is prevailing." In short, first
there is the proclamation of faith in a God who becomes
man and dies to save us, not doctrines and prohibitions.

Francis speaks about this in answering a question about
homosexual persons:

> We need to proclaim the Gospel on every street cor-
> ner, preaching the good news of the kingdom and heal-
> ing, even with our preaching, every kind of disease and
> wound. In Buenos Aires I used to receive letters from
> homosexual persons who are "socially wounded" be-
> cause they tell me that they feel like the Church has al-
> ways condemned them. But the Church does not want
> to do this. During the return flight from Rio de Janeiro

I said that if a homosexual person is of good will and is in search of God, I am no one to judge. By saying this, I said what the Catechism says. . . .

A person once asked me, in a provocative manner, if I approved of homosexuality. I replied with another question: "Tell me: when God looks at a gay person, does he endorse the existence of this person with love, or reject and condemn this person?" We must always consider the person. Here we enter into the mystery of the human being. In life, God accompanies persons, and we must accompany them, starting from their situation. It is necessary to accompany them with mercy. When that happens, the Holy Spirit inspires the priest to say the right thing.

Francis also declared:

Those who today always look for disciplinarian solutions, those who long for an exaggerated doctrinal "security", those who stubbornly try to recover a past that no longer exists—they have a static and inward-directed view of things. In this way, faith becomes an ideology among other ideologies. I have a dogmatic certainty: God is in every person's life. God is in everyone's life. Even if the life of a person has been a disaster, even if it is destroyed by vices, drugs, or anything else—God is in this person's life. You can, you must try to seek God in every human life. Although the life of a person is a land full of thorns and weeds, there is always a space in which the good seed can grow. You have to trust God.

~

LITTLE FLOWERS
OF FRUGALITY

~

That Gesture that Says:
"What? Are you kidding?"

> The culture of comfort . . . makes us insensitive
> to the cries of other people, makes us live in soap
> bubbles.
>
> *Homily in Lampedusa, July 8, 2013*

M any things in the Vatican changed with Francis.
Among them were the customary habits regarding the internal movements of the Pope, from one part to another of the smallest State in the world, with an area of less than half a square kilometer [0.17 square miles]. Before Bergoglio arrived, whenever the Pope traveled within the Vatican, internal traffic was blocked and access was closed off to visitors and to those who entered and exited the offices. The Pope traveled in a large black covered sedan.

From the evening of his election, Francis rejected the flagship of the Vatican fleet with the license plate "scv 1" (Italian for "Vatican City State 1"). After receiving the homage of the cardinals and blessing the crowd on St. Peter's Square, Bergoglio went down to the courtyard of San Damaso with his now former fellow prelates. And he found the big sedan ready for him, with the doors open. He was supposed to use it to return to the Domus Sanctae Marthae, the cardinals' residence during the conclave. Waiting for the prelates, on the other hand, were the white minibuses that had shuttled back and forth that day to transport the cardinals from St. Martha's to the historical site of the papal election, the Sistine Chapel, in the apostolic palace.

Francis did not take a moment to think. He did not even consider the flagship of the Vatican fleet of automobiles, which was considered more in keeping with his new "status". He resolutely headed toward the bus, in the company of the other cardinals. The scene was repeated the following morning, when Francis returned to the Sistine Chapel with the prelates to celebrate Mass: one of his traveling companions thought it would be a good idea to immortalize the incident with his mobile phone. The photo was published: it depicts Francis seated on the minibus, smiling alongside the Brazilian Cardinal Damasceno Assis, Archbishop of Aparecida.

Another example of the new Pontiff's determination occurred on Saturday, March 16, on the occasion of an audience granted to more than six thousand journalists accredited by the Vatican Press Office to cover the conclave. The audience was to take place in the Paul VI Auditorium, a few steps from the entrance to the Vatican off the *piazza* of the Holy Office and a few steps from the Domus Sanctae Marthae, the residence of the Pope.

In front of the entrance of the residence the automobile for the Pope had been stationed along with another car to escort it. All this just to travel less than a hundred meters [110 yards]. The policemen were there, the doors were open; waiting in front of the entrance were the Prefect of the Papal Household, Georg Gänswein, and his assistant, Leonardo Sapienza. Bergoglio appeared, looked at the gendarmes and the chauffeurs, smiled, and made an eloquent hand gesture as if to say, "But surely you don't think that I would get into a car to go a hundred meters." Then at his usual swift pace he headed alone toward the nearby Paul VI Auditorium for the audience, pursued by the Prefect and the Adjunct Prefect of the Papal Household, and also by the head of the Vatican Police, Domenico Giani. Meanwhile the cars remained parked where they were and the doors were closed.

Nowadays the Pope often travels on foot, whereas to travel to the apostolic palace he normally uses the blue Ford Focus. But all this happens in a much more relaxed atmosphere.

～

Black Shoes . . . with New Soles

Everyone has to live as the Lord asks him to live. But austerity—general austerity—I think it is necessary for all of us who work in the service of the Church.

Press Conference during the return flight from Rio de Janeiro, July 28, 2013

When fifty-six-year-old Bishop Eduardo Horacio García, Auxiliary Bishop and Vicar General of the Archdiocese of Buenos Aires, landed at Fiumicino Airport two days after the election of Pope Francis, he was carrying with him, among other things, a sealed shoebox. García was convinced that he was bringing to Bergoglio, who forty-eight hours earlier had been his Ordinary, a pair of new shoes, which the cardinal had acquired before leaving for the conclave.

In reality those shoes were not new. Virginia Bonar, a co-worker of Bergoglio in the Office of Social Communications of the Archdiocese of Buenos Aires, tells the story:

"They were delivered to the Pope by the Auxiliary Bishop, Bishop Eduardo García", the woman said during a television interview broadcast by the religion program of RaiUno, *A Sua Immagine* [In His Image], "to whom they had been entrusted in a sealed box. Thus he thought that he had brought the newly-elected Pope a pair of new shoes. But when the box was opened, he noticed that the shoes were the same ones as before; they had simply been resoled."

"Just as well that he bought himself a pair of shoes", the bishop had been telling himself. Instead Bishop García "told us then that the shoes were the old ones that Cardinal Bergoglio had left to be repaired before leaving for Rome." "It is nice to see that humility makes the news. You can start getting used to these gestures", Bergoglio's co-worker announced, "because they are typical of him." She was quite right.

Moreover from the evening of his election, Pope Francis refused to put on the red papal shoes and also to wear white zouave pants beneath his cassock, preferring instead to keep his old black trousers until they were worn out.

~

The Black Bag . . . of Normality

We cannot be Christians part-time. If Christ is at the center of our lives, he is present in all that we do.

@Pontifex (on Twitter), August 19, 2013

I t is an image that has circled the globe. On Monday morning, July 22, 2013, as his flight to Rio de Janeiro was about to depart from Fiumicino Airport, Pope Francis showed up carrying a black leather bag, his carry-on luggage. Bergoglio arrived by helicopter from Vatican City. He found the Italian Prime Minister, Enrico Letta, there to welcome him. The Pope descended from the helicopter, greeted Letta and the other civil and ecclesiastical authorities, while still holding his baggage in his left hand. The black bag was quite visible at the moment when Francis slowly climbed the stairs and boarded the Alitalia airplane which was to carry him and his entourage (including journalists) to Brazil for the World Youth Day celebrations.

The photo of the Pontiff boarding the airplane with his briefcase in hand was posted by online daily news websites and reprinted by many, many newspapers throughout the world. Many authoritative commentators endeavored to analyze the significance of this gesture. Some journalists tried to guess what the Pope's carry-on bag contained that was so important that he could not be separated from it. Maybe important documents concerning the reform of the Roman Curia? Perhaps the most explosive dossiers about the infamous Vatileaks incident?

The following week, right after leaving Brazil to return to Rome, Pope Francis responded for about an hour and a half to questions of the journalists who were flying with him: it was a genuine press conference without networks and without prepared questions. A journalist asked the Pope why he carried his luggage personally, what was in that bag that had prompted such speculations. He was informed of the fact that the photo of him with briefcase in hand had been published everywhere to the great surprise of many. Indeed, no one had ever seen a Pope who carried his baggage by himself: in addition to his personal secretary, the Pontiff has at his side the Adjutant Chamberlain, who is specifically responsible for that.

With a smile on his face, surprised in turn by the interest aroused by this detail, Francis replied as follows:

It wasn't the key for the atom bomb! Well! I was carrying it because that's what I've always done. When I travel, I carry it. And inside, what was there? There was a razor, a breviary, an appointment book, a book to read, I brought one about St. Thérèse, to whom I have a devotion. I have always taken a bag with me when traveling—it's normal. But we must be normal . . . I don't know . . . what you say is a bit strange for me, that the photograph went all over the world. But we must get used to being normal. The normality of life.

Less striking and above all less photographed was another detail. On August 28, Francis went to celebrate Mass in the Basilica of St. Augustine in Campo Marzio, on the occasion of the opening of the 184th General Chapter of the Augustinian Order and on the feast day of the saintly Bishop of Hippo.

The Pope was photographed while getting out of the car; he was carrying under his arm, in the white fabric container designed for the purpose, the miter that he would wear during the liturgy. "We must get used to being normal."

～

In Flight but without the Bed

There is no such thing as low-cost Christianity.
Following Jesus means swimming against the tide,
renouncing evil and selfishness.

@Pontifex (on Twitter), September 5, 2013

Where do the passengers normally board? In Fiumicino? Then I do not want to cause inconvenience by leaving from Ciampino. . . ." These were the words spoken by Pope Francis when the logistics of his first foreign trip, the pilgrimage to Brazil, to Rio de Janeiro, on the occasion of the World Youth Day celebrations were explained to him. The Pope chose to depart from Fiumicino Airport and not from Ciampino, as had initially been planned in advance. Another reason was because during the summer he stayed in the Vatican and did not go to spend the vacation at Castel Gandolfo, a locality from which it is more convenient to reach the airport in Ciampino.

The Pope informed the airline Alitalia that he did not want any special internal accommodations on the flight. He traveled seated in a first-class reclining chair [*poltrona*], but without the installation of the bed that in the past had been prepared for the Pontiff during long intercontinental flights.

For Bergoglio, this first-class seat was already a luxury compared with his usual practice. As a cardinal—the journalist Evangelina Himitian discovered—he had in fact customarily traveled economy class, and he continued to do so even after he developed hip problems; he used to ask about the availability of economy-class seats on the aisle next to the emergency exit, which would allow him to stretch out his legs. He did this even on Tuesday, February 26, 2013, when he departed from Buenos Aires on a flight to Rome, where he was to participate in the conclave that on March 13 elected him Pope, preventing him from using his return ticket.

These requests were communicated to the airline in time, before it was decided and announced which airplane would transport the Pope and his entourage to Brazil. Francis' request in advance proved to be manna from heaven for Alitalia: the designs of its airplanes in fact no longer allow the possibility of providing special accommodations within a reasonably short time. The work to prepare the bed would have taken too long and would have been considerably more difficult than was the case in the past with less extensively wired and computerized airplanes and seating.

This request by the Pontiff was denied by some Vatican sources. But Francis himself confirmed it in the press conference held on the airplane during the return flight from Rio de Janeiro to Rome. Answering a question from the journalist Jean-Marie Guénois from *Le Figaro*, Bergoglio declared:

This plane doesn't have any special arrangements. I am up front, I have a nice seat, a normal one, the same as everyone else has. I had them write a letter and make a phone call to say that I did not want special arrangements on the plane: is that clear?

∼

A Pope with a Bus Bass

The Church is all of us: from the baby just baptized to the Bishop, the Pope; we are all the Church and we are all equal in the eyes of God!

General Audience, September 11, 2013

B ut does it really work?" was Pope Francis' question when Roberto Diacetti, the administrator delegated by ATAC, the public transportation agency of Rome, presented him with a bus pass. Certainly, the gift was packaged in a leather case, and the pass was special, white—as is fitting for a Pope—with the Vatican coat of arms on the back (a "logo" that obviously is not found on normal ATAC passes). But the delegated administrator immediately reassured the Bishop of Rome: this was not a collector's item or a precious souvenir. The pass works, and there is no time limit on it. "We designed it especially for you; it is valid on all the transportation lines of Rome, even though it is one of a kind. You can use it to take any public transportation", Roberto Diacetti explained to Francis.

The Pope looked at the little white plastic rectangle again and again and replied: "Maybe I could even use it. . . ." "But I think that they will not allow me to take a spin", he added facetiously, gesturing with a visible movement of his head toward the men responsible for his safety.

In Buenos Aires, as an auxiliary bishop and then as archbishop and cardinal, Jorge Mario Bergoglio almost always traveled on foot or by bus. "I met Bergoglio for the first time in April 2001", says Francesca Ambrogetti, co-author with Sergio Rubin of a book-length interview with the future Pope, "right after the consistory in which John Paul II had named him a cardinal. I invited him to a meeting with the foreign press. I remember that on the telephone I told him that I would send a car to pick him up, and he replied, 'No, tell me where it is; I will take the bus.' I was not expecting that answer. He arrived dressed as a simple priest. I remember wondering: is that he, or one of his assistants?"

In Rome, too, Bergoglio always traveled on foot or by public transportation. From his residence in the Domus Internationalis Paolo VI on Via della Scrofa at the Vatican, he used to walk through the alleys of the town. At a swift gait. And now that he has become Bishop of the Eternal City? "You know how often I've wanted to go walking through the streets of Rome", he replied a bit nostalgically to a question during the press conference on his return flight from Rio de Janeiro. "Because, in Buenos Aires, I liked to go for a walk in the city." He continued:

I really liked to do that! In this sense, I feel a little penned in. But I have to say one thing, and that is that these fellows from the Vatican Gendarmerie are so good, they are really, really good, and I am grateful to them. Now they're letting me do a few more things! I think . . . their job is to maintain security. So, penned in, in that sense. I'd like to go out walking but I understand that it isn't possible: I understand. That was what I meant. Because I used to be—as we say in Buenos Aires—a *callejero*, a street priest. . . .

In other words, a priest accustomed to walking through the streets.

And therefore, now that he is Pope, he would like to continue walking alone or else being a passenger on the bus and on the subway. Maybe that was another reason why he did not turn down the invitation from the ATAC administrator who, as he presented him with an unlimited "Metrebus" pass, told him: "Well, then, if you approve, we can invite you to the grand opening of the new Metro C. That would be a great honor for us to be able to count on your presence." "Yes, I would like that. I look forward to the invitation", was Francis' response. There had never been a "Pope pass" before, the Roman daily newspaper *Il Messagero* notes; this is the first unlimited transpass given to a Pontiff. "The idea came to us when we learned that the Holy Father used to take public transportation in Argentina", the ATAC administrator explains.

The Roman transportation authority had already paid homage to the Argentine Pope immediately after his election by printing two hundred thousand tickets welcoming him. They bore the image of Pope Francis greeting the crowd from the balcony of St. Peter's at his first appearance. The tickets went on sale on March 27 at the subway stations and in around two hundred retail shops in center-city Rome.

"Let rulers be humble"

The future demands a rehabilitation of politics here
and now, a rehabilitation of politics, which is one of
the highest forms of charity.

Address to Brazilian leaders,
Rio de Janeiro, July 27, 2013

S omeone who governs must have the virtues of "humility" and "love" for the people. And good Catholics should "immerse themselves in politics". This is what
Pope Francis said in the homily during the Mass that he
celebrated at the Domus Sanctae Marthae on September
16, 2013, commenting on the Gospel reading about the
centurion who humbly asks for the healing of his servant,
and the Letter of St. Paul to Timothy with its exhorta-
tion to pray for rulers. Passages which Bergoglio used to
explain the "service of authority". Several excerpts from
the homily were broadcast by Vatican Radio.

Someone who governs, Francis said, "must love his
people", because "A ruler who does not love cannot govern. At most he can only make a bit of order, but he
cannot govern." "It is not possible to govern without
love for the people and without humility!" the Pope explained.

All men and women who assume the responsibility of
governing should ask themselves these two questions:
"Do I love my people, so that I may better serve them?"
And "am I humble enough to hear the opinions of others so as to choose the best way of governing?" If they
do not ask themselves these questions, they will not
govern well. The ruler, man or woman, who loves the
people is a humble man or woman.

These words are a thousand miles away from the strate-
gic politics of holding on to power or furthering personal
interests. These words put the "common good" back at
the center.

But Bergoglio, echoing St. Paul who exhorts the citi-
zens to offer prayers for "all who are in high positions,
that we may lead a quiet and peaceable life", recalled that
we cannot be apathetic about politics. "No one can say:
'I do not get involved in that; they rule.' No, no; I am responsible for their rule, and I must do my best to see that
they rule well, and I must do my best by participating in
politics insofar as I am able. Politics—the Social Teaching of the Church tells us—is one of the highest forms
of charity, because it serves the common good. I cannot
wash my hands of it, can I? We all must do something!"

Francis then observed that it has become very common to say only bad things about rulers, complaining
about "things that are not going well". "You listen to the
television and they criticize and find fault. You read the
newspapers and they criticize. Always the bad things, always opposition!" Maybe—the Pontiff continued—"the
ruler is indeed a sinner, as David was, but I must coop-
erate with my opinion, with my voice, and also with my

correction", because everyone "must participate in the common good!" And he added that although "we have heard it said so often: 'A good Catholic does not get mixed up in politics', that is not true; that is not a good path." Bergoglio explained:

A good Catholic immerses himself in politics, by offering the best of himself, so that the leader can govern. But what is the best thing that we can offer to those who govern? Prayer! Therefore let us give our best, our ideas and suggestions, our best, but the best thing of all is prayer. Let us pray for our leaders that they may govern us well, that they may bring about progress in our homeland, our nations, our world, so as to achieve peace and the common good.

The Pastor Who Did Not
Want to Become a Bishop

Being a bishop . . . in Buenos Aires I was very happy, very happy! And as Pope: likewise! When the Lord puts you there, if you do what the Lord wants, you are happy.

Press conference on the return flight from
Rio de Janeiro, July 28, 2013

P ope Francis has criticized several times the influence of a worldly mentality in the Church. On the other hand, on May 17, 2013, during the homily at the morning Mass that he celebrated at the Domus Sanctae Marthae, he related another incident that occurred in the confessional, although in this case he did not refer it directly to his experience as a confessor. Nevertheless we cannot rule out the possibility that he was speaking about something that had happened to him personally.

"Once," he related, "I knew a priest, a good pastor who did good work; he was appointed bishop, and he was ashamed because he did not feel worthy; it tormented him spiritually. And he went to his confessor. The confessor listened to him and told him: 'Do not be alarmed. If after the big sin that Peter committed they made him

Pope, you go right ahead!' And he said that the Lord is like that. The Lord is like that. The Lord makes us mature by many encounters with him, even with our weaknesses, when we acknowledge them, along with our sins. . . ."

These are comforting words, not only because they show us that there are candidates to the episcopate who feel unworthy and consider declining (when what one usually finds is careerism), but also and above all because of that commemoration of Peter's betrayal. The man to whom Jesus said "on this Rock I will build my Church" is the one who denied him three times.

LITTLE FLOWERS OF
EVERYDAY HOLINESS

~

The Holiness of Patient People

God calls each of us to be holy, to live his life, but he has a particular path for each one of us.

Address to World Youth Day volunteers, July 28, 2013

I n his interview with *La Civiltà Cattolica* that was published in English in *America* magazine, the Pope said:

I see holiness in the patience of the people of God: a woman who is raising children, a man who works to bring home the bread, the sick, the elderly priests who have so many wounds but have a smile on their faces because they served the Lord, the sisters who work hard and live a hidden sanctity. This is for me the common sanctity. I often associate sanctity with patience: not only patience as . . . taking charge of the events and circumstances of life, but also as a constancy in going forward, day by day. This is the sanctity of the Church Militant also mentioned by St. Ignatius. This was the sanctity of my parents: my dad, my mom, my grandmother Rosa who loved me so much.

In my breviary I have the last will of my grandmother Rosa, and I read it often. For me it is like a prayer. She is a saint who has suffered so much, also spiritually, and yet always went forward with courage.

In that last will, which even today has a place among the worn pages of Bergoglio's breviary, his grandmother wrote:

> May these, my grandchildren, to whom I gave the best of my heart, have a long, happy life, but if someday sorrow, sickness, or the loss of a beloved person should fill them with distress, let them remember that a sigh directed toward the Tabernacle, where the greatest and noblest martyr is, and a look at Mary at the foot of the cross, can make a drop of balm fall on the deepest and most painful wounds.

The Grandmother Quoted
in the Homilies

How important grandparents are for family life, for
passing on the human and religious heritage which
is so essential for each and every society!

Angelus, Archbishop's Residence,
Rio de Janeiro, July 26, 2013

A s is now almost always his custom, being a pastor
who is used to preaching off the cuff, Pope Francis
often looks up from his prepared text and improvises. So
it happened on St. Peter's Square on Palm Sunday also,
when Pope Francis mentioned "greed for money" as one
of the "wounds" that are "inflicted upon humanity by
evil" and added: "My grandmother always used to tell
us children: a shroud has no pockets!" We must leave
the goods that we have accumulated here; they do not
accompany us on our final voyage. Thus, although it is
somewhat unusual for a Papal Mass, the Pontiff's grandmother was quoted in the homily.

Francis was referring to his father's *mamma*, Rosa Marg-
herita Vassallo, born in 1884 in Val Bormida, married
in Turin to Giovanni Bergoglio. From their union was

born in 1908 the Pope's father, Mario. In January 1929 the Bergoglio family, after departing from Portacomaro, landed in Buenos Aires to rejoin other relatives who had already emigrated to Argentina. Signora Rosa, despite the hot, humid air—in the southern hemisphere it is midsummer in January—was wearing a coat with a fur collar, completely out of place in that temperature. In the lining of the coat was the money from the sale of the family property.

Little Jorge, born in December 1936, grew up spending part of the day at the house of his grandparents, who handed down to him a bit of the Piedmontese dialect and most importantly the Christian faith. In a radio interview granted in November 2012 to the radio station of the parish of Villa 21 of Barracas, one of the poor districts of Buenos Aires, the future Pope had said: "The one who taught me to pray was my grandmother. She gave me a lot of instruction in the faith and told me the stories of the saints."

Several years ago, in an interview on the television network EWTN, Cardinal Bergoglio had recalled:

> Once, when I was in the seminary, my grandmother told me: "Never forget that you are about to become a priest and that the most important thing for a priest is to celebrate the Mass", and she told me about a mother who said to her son, who was a truly holy priest, "Celebrate the Mass, every Mass, as though it were your first and your last."

In the book-length interview *The Jesuit*, the future Pope had related how he kept folded up in his breviary, the two-volume prayer book he always carries with him, even during his travels, a letter from his grandmother—a kind of short last will and testament that she left for her grandchildren.

On May 3, 2013, Francis again quoted his grandmother in a homily during the daily Mass that he celebrated at the Domus Sanctae Marthae. He recalled that she had been the one to transmit to him his faith in the Resurrection. Every year *Nonna* Rosa accompanied her grandchildren to the "procession of the candles". He remembered that always "at the end of the procession came [the statue of] Christ lying in the tomb, and our grandmother made us kneel down and told us children: 'Look, he is dead, but tomorrow he will be risen!'"

The Holiness of a Mother

Christians know that suffering cannot be eliminated, yet it can have meaning and become an act of love and . . . a moment of growth in faith and love.

Lumen Fidei, 56

T he telephone call came thanks to a few words scrawled on a paper towel. A few lines imbued with suffering and courage. In September [2013], a cleaning woman who worked at the airport in Buenos Aires happened to learn that the man who had just walked by was the head of a Catholic television station and was about to board a direct flight to Rome where he would meet Pope Francis. A chance meeting, a few words heard in passing. And she went ahead and decided to write a brief message, to tell about her addicted, unemployed son, to say that she worked every day hoping that he could escape the nightmare of drugs. That she was working for him, dedicating her life to him. That she toiled for many hours a day, dreaming of a better future for him.

On the paper towel the woman dashed off a few sentences asking the Pope to remember them in prayer, and she entrusted it to the journalist. That unique missive on a napkin crossed the ocean and arrived in Bergoglio's hands. The journalist passed along that torn piece of paper, and two days after receiving it, on Sunday, September 15, Francis telephoned the woman and asked to speak to the son as well. He listened to both of them and said that he was close to them and was praying for them. The next day, while meeting the priests of Rome, his clergy, Francis cited that mother's request: this was the only case so far of a papal telephone call revealed by the caller and not by the recipient. Bergoglio pointed out to the priests the example of the woman and said: "Isn't that holiness?" The Church "does not collapse", he added, because even today "there is great holiness in the Church: there are many women and many men who live their faith in everyday life."

"The Church", Bergoglio said, "is a mother who is not afraid to go into the night, to give hope. . . . The Church is a merciful mother who always seeks to encourage." The red thread that connects them? Situations of pain, suffering, and solitude but also of courage and determination.

To the Brazilian bishops, Pope Francis had said that it is necessary to recover the "grammar of simplicity": what is needed is a Church "capable of accompanying" and of "warming hearts". Through these telephone calls, and the many others that we will never know about, the Pope as "pastor" entered into the individual lives of normal persons. Extraordinarily normal people, just like him.

～

"The Church is not a babysitter"

The security of faith does not make us motionless
or close us off, but sends us forth to bear witness and
to dialogue with all people.

@Pontifex (on Twitter), August 2, 2013

The Church cannot and must never become like "a
babysitter who cares for the child just to get him
to sleep". If that happened, she would be "a slumbering
Church". Pope Francis said this on April 17, 2013, in
his homily during the Mass that he celebrated in the Domus Sanctae Marthae. With these words the Pope tried
to explain that someone who has come to know Jesus has
the strength and the courage to proclaim him; someone
who has received baptism has the strength to walk, to go
forward and to evangelize. And "when we do this the
Church becomes a mother who generates children" who
are capable of bringing Jesus to the world.

During his homily Francis, commenting on the first
reading taken from the Acts of the Apostles, recalled that
"after the martyrdom of Stephen, a violent persecution
against the Church of Jerusalem broke out. We read in the
book of Acts that the Church was quite calm, quite peace-
ful, with charity among them; the widows were cared

for. But then persecution arrived. This is, as it were, the lifestyle of the Church: [alternating] between the peace of charity and persecution."

This happens, Francis added, because it happened that way in the life of Jesus. As a result of persecution, they all fled, except for the Apostles. The Christians, on the other hand, "went: alone. Without priests. Without bishops: alone. The bishops, the apostles, were in Jerusalem putting up a little resistance to these persecutions." Nevertheless those who had fled "went from place to place, proclaiming the Word."

And the Pope wanted to focus our attention on them. They, indeed,

left their houses; maybe they brought a few things with them. They had no security but went from place to place proclaiming the Gospel. They brought with them the only true wealth they had: the faith. The gift that they had received from the Lord. They were simple believers, just baptized a year before or maybe a little less than that. But they had the courage to go forth and to proclaim. And they were believed! And they even worked miracles. "Unclean spirits came out of many who were possessed, crying with a loud voice; and many who were paralyzed or lame were healed."

"So there was much joy in that city." Philip had also gone. Those Christians—recent Christians—had the strength, the courage to proclaim Jesus. They proclaimed him with their words, but also with their life. They aroused curiosity: "But who are these people?" And they said: "We have come to know Jesus, we have found Jesus and are bringing him." They had only the strength of baptism. And baptism gave them that apostolic courage, the strength of the Spirit.

Francis then compared that example of the first preaching to the contemporary situation. "I wonder whether we baptized Christians have that strength. And I wonder: 'Do we believe in this? That baptism is sufficient to evangelize? Or do we hope that the priest will talk, that the bishop will talk. . . . And what about us?'"

Too often, the Pope remarked, the grace of baptism "is left aside" and we end up being confined in our thoughts, in our concerns. "Sometimes we think: 'No, we are Christians: we have received baptism, we have been confirmed, made our First Communion . . . and so the identification card is okay. And now, let us sleep peacefully: we are Christians.' But where is that strength of the Spirit that brings you forward?"

"Are we faithful to the Spirit so as to proclaim Christ by our lives, by our witness, and by our words?" the Pope asked. "When we do this, the Church becomes a mother who generates children. But", Francis warned, "when we do not do it, the Church becomes not a mother but a babysitter, who cares for the child just to get him to sleep. This is a slumbering Church. Let us think about our baptism, about the responsibility of our baptism."

To give a concrete example, Pope Francis recalled an incident that happened in Japan in the first decades of the seventeenth century, when the Catholic missionaries were expelled from the country and the communities remained without priests for more than two centuries. When the missionaries returned, they found a lively community in which everyone was baptized, catechized, and married in the Church! And even those who had died had received a Christian burial. "But there was no priest! Who had done all that? The baptized!" This is the great responsibility of the baptized: "To proclaim Christ, to promote the Church, that fruitful motherhood of the Church. To be Christian is not to make a career out of studying to become a Christian lawyer or doctor; no. To be Christian is a gift that makes us walk forward with the strength of the Spirit in proclaiming Jesus Christ."

∼

A God Who Goes Ahead of Us

Yesterday I celebrated the sixtieth anniversary of the
day when I heard Jesus' voice in my heart. . . . I have
not regretted it because always, . . . I have looked at
Jesus and trusted in him and he has not deserted me.

Address to young people, Cagliari,
September 22, 2013

The vocation of Jorge Mario Bergoglio was manifested as a call of which it is possible to determine
the day and the hour. The one directly concerned speaks
of it as an event that turned his life upside down. Something that burst in unexpected. A God who comes to seek
you before you seek him.

The future pope was seventeen years old and was
preparing to celebrate "Student Day", a holiday at the
beginning of spring, that is, in the Southern hemisphere,
September 21. With his school friends he planned to go
on a picnic. But the day had taken a completely different
turn. Jorge actually went to his parish church of San José
de Flores. There was no particular reason for that visit.
And yet a decisive encounter occurred. He found there
a priest whom he had never met before, Fr. Duarte, who

conveyed to him a deep spirituality. The young man decided to make his confession to him, and during that confession, Jorge Mario "discovered" his religious vocation. He became aware of the fact that he had been called. Something happened that changed his life. To such an extent that he decided not to meet with his friends who were waiting for him at the railroad station. He went back home instead, because in his heart he had decided to become a priest.

"During that confession something unusual happened to me, I cannot say what, but it was something that changed my life. I would say that it was as though I had been surprised while my guard was down", Bergoglio told the journalists Rubin and Ambrogetti.

> It was the surprise, the amazement of an encounter, I realized that they were waiting for me. This is the religious experience: the amazement of meeting someone who is expecting you. From that moment on, God became for me the One who goes ahead of you. One is seeking him and he seeks you first. One wants to meet him, but he comes to meet us first.

But Bergoglio adds another characteristic that was destined to become the heart of his ministry as a priest, a bishop, and now as Pope. Indeed, it was not just "the amazement of an encounter" at the origin of his religious vocation, but also the merciful way in which God had called him.

His entrance into the seminary did not occur immediately after that call. In fact four more years would pass.

The decision was made, but was kept in his heart, protected and cultivated. "The matter ended there for the moment", he confirms. Jorge continued to work in the testing lab, completed his studies, and did not yet speak with anyone about his desire to become a priest. "I had a wilderness experience, a 'passive solitude' of the sort that is endured without any apparent reason or because of a crisis or a loss." It is as though this upsetting call, accompanied by the experience of mercy, had needed to mature.

～

Women and the Resurrection

Faith is . . . a gift from God given to us in the Church and through the Church.

General Audience, September 11, 2013

T he first witnesses of the Resurrection were wo-men. . . . In the Church and on the journey of faith, [women] had and still have today a special role in opening the doors to the Lord."

In his second General Audience on St. Peter's Square, Pope Francis spoke about the resurrection of Jesus and about the Gospel accounts that describe it, noting that "the first witnesses of this event were the women." At dawn of that first day after the Sabbath, the Pope recalled, they went to the tomb and found it empty, and then met the messenger from God who announced the resurrection.

The women were motivated by love and were able to accept this announcement with faith: they believed and passed it on straight away, they did not keep it to themselves but passed it on. . . . In the profession of faith in the New Testament only men are recorded as witnesses of the Resurrection, the Apostles, but not the women. This is because, according to the Judaic Law of that time, women and children could not bear a trustworthy, credible witness.

Instead in the Gospels women play a fundamental lead role. Here we can grasp an element in favour of the historicity of the Resurrection: if it was an invented event, in the context of that time it would not have been linked with the evidence of women. Instead the Evangelists simply recounted what happened: women were the first witnesses. This implies that God does not choose in accordance with human criteria: the first witnesses of the birth of Jesus were shepherds, simple, humble people; the first witnesses of the Resurrection were women. And this is beautiful.

Bergoglio then added extemporaneously:

This is part of the mission of women; of mothers, of women! Witnessing to their children, to their grandchildren, that Jesus is alive, is living, is risen. Mothers and women, carry on witnessing to this! It is the heart that counts for God, how open to him we are, whether we are like trusting children. However this also makes us think about how women, in the Church and on the journey of faith, had and still have today a special role in opening the doors to the Lord, in following him and in communicating his Face, for the gaze of faith is always in need of the simple and profound gaze of love. The Apostles and disciples find it harder to believe. The women, not so.

In his catechesis the Pope referred to a conclusion that many biblical scholars have arrived at. "All scholars should agree", wrote Xavier Léon-Dufour, "that the narrative of the visit of the women to the tomb is not, originally at least, apologetic in purpose. If it was, why should women have been chosen as witnesses, since according to Jewish custom, they were not qualified to give legal testimony?" The female word that no Hebrew tribunal would have accepted as valid became the daily support of the faith of the first Christians.

∾

The White Rose of St. Thérèse

True peace, that profound peace, comes from experiencing God's mercy.

Regina Coeli, April 7, 2013

On Sunday, September 8, the day after the long prayer vigil for peace in Syria, during which several passages from the writings of St. Thérèse of Lisieux had been read, Pope Francis received as a surprise gift a white rose. A flower that for him is a "sign" connected specifically to devotion to that saint. The one who revealed this, with the authorization of Francis himself, was the Archbishop of Ancona-Osimo, Edoardo Menichelli. The prelate, to whom the incident had been recounted by Bergoglio on the preceding day, mentioned it publicly in the course of the presentation of a book that had arrived from Pedaso, in the province of Fermo. The book, published by Lindau, is entitled *Teresa di Lisieux: Il fascino della santità: I segreti di una dottrina ritrovata* [Thérèse of Lisieux: The charm of holiness: Secrets of a rediscovered doctrine]; it is a voluminous and well-documented study by Gianni Gennari, which the Pontiff had brought with him in his briefcase during his journey to Brazil in July.

Archbishop Menichelli related: "The Pope told me that he had been surprised, while strolling in the Vatican gardens on Sunday, September 8, by a gardener who presented to him a white rose that he had just picked. He considers this flower a 'sign', a 'message' from St. Thérèse, to whom he had turned anxiously the preceding day." The archbishop conveyed Francis' greeting to those present, telling them that he had been authorized by the Pope to speak also about the incident of the white rose. The Pope did not make a connection between the white rose and the vigil for peace the evening before. But it is not difficult to imagine that among the worries of the Bishop of Rome was specifically the international situation, the massacres in Syria, the much-debated intervention of the Western bombers.

What is the significance of the white rose for Bergoglio? He himself spoke about it, as a cardinal, in the book-length interview *The Jesuit* written by Sergio Rubin and Francesca Ambrogetti. In describing Bergoglio's library in Buenos Aires, the two journalists note:

> Our gaze caught on a vase brimming with white roses on one of the shelves in his library, with an image of St. Thérèse of Lisieux behind it. "Whenever I have a problem," he told us, "I ask the saint not to resolve it, but to take it in her hands and help me accept it, and, as a sign, I almost always receive a white rose."

The Pope's devotion to the Carmelite mystic, who died at the age of twenty-four in 1897, was canonized by Pius XI and was proclaimed a Doctor of the Church by Pope John Paul II in 1997, is well known. Francis himself had spoken about it to the journalists on his return flight from Rio de Janeiro. Thérèse, while she was still alive, had promised that after her death she would shower down from heaven "rose petals", that is, graces granted by God through her intercession. She wrote: "A soul inflamed with love cannot remain inactive. . . . If only you knew what I plan to do when I am in heaven . . . I will spend my heaven by doing good on earth." So during the vigil on September 7, the mysteries of the rosary were recited, alternating with passages from the Gospel and verses from a poem by the saint from Lisieux.

This devotion and the message of the roses did not start with Bergoglio. On December 3, 1925, Fr. Putigan, a Jesuit, began a novena to pray for a very important grace. He also asked for a sign, so as to know whether his prayers had been answered. He asked to receive a rose as a gift. He spoke to no one about the novena or about the unusual request he had made to the saint. Then, on the third day of the novena, he received the rose that he had requested, and therefore the grace. He then started another novena. On the fourth day of this second novena, a nun who belonged to a nursing order brought him a white rose and told him: "St. Thérèse is sending you this rose." So the Jesuit decided to spread the word about what he called the "miraculous rose novena", which from then on spread throughout the world.

LITTLE FLOWERS
ON THE TELEPHONE

~

"Hello? This is Francis.
Tell me about yourself. . . ."

It is useless to ask a seriously injured person if he has high cholesterol and about the level of his blood sugars! You have to heal his wounds. Then we can talk about everything else.

Interview with La Civiltà Cattolica, *September 19, 2013*

Hello, *Michele*, this is Pope Francis. . . ." At the other end of the line, Michele Ferri, age forty, had just answered the phone, curious about the completely unfamiliar caller number. His brother, Andrea, the owner of several gas stations, had been killed on June 3, 2013, by one of his employees, aided by an accomplice. A brutal crime, and a wound that does not heal. "I have always forgiven you for everything. Not this time, God; I don't forgive you for this", Michele wrote on the social network. But the victim's brother did not just post his grief on Facebook. He took pen and paper and wrote to the Pope, telling him about his suffering.

Even though Michele knew that a Pope who likes normality now sits in the Vatican, he certainly was not expecting that telephone call. Michele himself, who for years has been wheelchair-bound, spoke about it on his Facebook profile: "Today I had an unexpected phone call. . . . When I said 'Hello?', a voice answered, saying, 'Hello, Michele, this is Pope Francis. . . .' I was so excited!" His post went on to say: "He told me that he cried when he read the letter that I had written to him." A few days later, as he had promised Michele he would do, the Pope also telephoned his mother, Rosalba Tomassoni. He conversed with her for ten minutes, comforting her and noting that they had both been born in the same year, in 1936.

Another person who has received a telephone call from the Pope is a nineteen-year-old engineering student in Padua, Stefano Cabizza. It all started on the Feast of the Assumption in 2013, when Stefano, together with his family, participated in the Mass celebrated by the Pope in Castel Gandolfo, on the plaza in front of the papal palace. The young man had brought with him also a letter in the hope that he could deliver it to Francis. "Honestly, I did not think that I would succeed", the young man admitted; instead he entrusted it to one of the priests who were distributing Communion to the faithful.

A few days later, unexpectedly, a personal response arrived from Pope Francis, who wanted to speak to the young man directly. He is an average youth, an avid soccer fan, who in his letter had not referred to any particular tragedies or experiences that he had been through. He just wanted to get acquainted with him and speak with him, even about faith.

Stefano told the daily newspaper *Il Gazzettino* that Bergoglio called the youth's house twice. Indeed, the first time there was no answer. "Hello, who is there?" "Hello, this is Pope Francis. Tell me about yourself." In response to the young man's astonishment—he went on to report —Bergoglio told him: "Do you think that the apostles addressed Jesus formally? Or that they called him Your Excellency? They were friends, as you and I are now, and with my friends I am used to saying *tu* [the familiar pronoun]."

"The Pope", Cabizza related, "asked me to pray a lot to St. Stephen and to pray also for him. He gave me his blessing, and I felt great strength within me. He gave me the determination to believe in myself to the end." The conversation lasted eight minutes. "It was the most beautiful day of my life" for the young student, who explains that he decided to talk about his "fantastic experience" only "to highlight Pope Francis' gesture of great humility and his closeness to us, the lay faithful."

Francis spoke specifically about this phone call with Fr. Antonio Spadaro in his interview with *La Civiltà Cattolica* [reprinted in English in *America* magazine].

I saw [that the] newspapers [gave a lot of attention to] the phone call I made to a young man who wrote me a letter. I called him because that letter was so beautiful, so simple. For me this was an act of generativity. I realized that he was a young man who is growing, that he saw in me a father, and that the letter tells something of his life to that father. The father cannot say, "I do not care." This type of fruitfulness is so good for me.

Especially moving is the story of Alejandra Pereyra, a forty-four-year-old Argentine woman, the victim of a rape by a policeman, who on August 25, 2013, spoke with the Pope by telephone for almost a half hour. "When I heard his voice it seemed to me that I was touched by the hand of God."

Alejandra related her experience to Channel 10 of the radio-television network of the National University of Córdova (UNC), saying that she had written an e-mail message to the Pontiff ten days earlier to ask for help and to complain of having been the victim of injustice twice: first as a victim of a rape by a policeman and then, after she filed a complaint, as the object of continual threats, harassment, and investigations. "Yesterday at 3:50 P.M. my cell phone rang, and when I asked who it was, I heard the answer: 'The Pope.' I was petrified." It was "a conversation about faith and trust. Francis listened very attentively to my story. Now I am doing everything I can to go to the Vatican. He told me that he would receive me in an audience."

"Now I know that I am not alone and I will get back on my feet. The Pope told me that I am not alone and he asked me to have confidence in the justice system", Alejandra reports. "Francis told me that he received thousands of letters every day, but that what I had written to him had moved him deeply and had touched his heart."

Among the many breaches of protocol to which Francis has become accustomed there are the telephone calls that the Pope makes directly, without intermediaries or secretaries. Gradually this habit of making papal phone calls should stop making the news. Bergoglio used to communicate in this way in Buenos Aires too, and so when he was just elected, on that very evening of March 13, he called at home two families of friends whom he had been accustomed to visit when he came to Rome. Then he personally called his local newsstand to tell them that because of his new position in Rome he would no longer be a subscriber to the daily newspaper *La Nación*. And it took a while to convince the owner that it was not a prank call but that he really was the Pope.

Francis also called his dentist in the Argentine capital to cancel an appointment that he had made, which he would not be able to keep because something more important had come up: he had to stay in the Vatican. On the telephone he spoke with the secretary, who at first could not believe her ears. He has made personal calls to friends, and also to priests and lay persons who have written to him. He once called someone to thank him for sending a book. And he does this without ever being introduced by a secretary.

A Pope who telephones inevitably causes astonishment. Monsignor Dario Viganò, director of the Vatican Television Center, had the opportunity during an audience to ask the Pope directly for a few more details. And Francis looked at him, astonished: "Tell the journalists that my telephone calls are not news", he explained to him. "That is how I am; I always did this in Buenos Aires too. I would receive a note, a letter from a priest in difficulty, a family, or a prisoner, and I would respond. For me it is much simpler to call, to find out about the problem and to suggest a solution, if there is one. Some I telephone, to others I write instead." Then, Viganò told the magazine *Famiglia Cristiana*, the Pope concluded with amusement, "It is better that they do not know all the things that I have done!"

∽

The Pope's Renault 4

There are many people in need in today's world. Am I self-absorbed in my own concerns or am I aware of those who need help?

@Pontifex (on Twitter), September 17, 2013

On Saturday afternoon, September 7, Francis was photographed getting into an old white Renault 4. The new evangelical-poverty-model popemobile? The website of the magazine *Famiglia Cristiana* revealed how and why Bergoglio was immortalized in that economy car.

The car is a 1984 Renault 4, with Italian license plate "Verona 779684". "The great thing", the Italian Catholic weekly publication writes, "is that this economy car has a 300,000-kilometer-long history of charitable travels" [approx. 190,000 miles]. The car used to belong to Fr. Renzo Zocca, today the pastor of Santa Lucia di Pescantina in Verona. "It was sitting in a garage in a slightly battered state, even though the priest had had it checked and certified as a vintage car. Fr. Renzo, who turns seventy in November, has ministered among the marginalized and is the founder of social cooperative *Àncora* [Anchor of

Hope], which provides many people with jobs and assistance. His outreach was to the working class neighborhood of Saval in Verona, where he served as parish priest in the 1980s."

Fr. Renzo fought barehanded against drug dealers who were destroying the lives of youngsters in his flock and used to send him death threats. He was even stabbed once, but he carried on, remaining in his "trench" and proclaiming the Gospel. "I wanted to be an embodiment of the Council in that marginalized parish that was the center of my life: I have spent twenty-five years there. My brother and I lived in an apartment on the ninth floor: I used to joke that I had the loftiest rectory in all of Italy."

The white Renault 4 was given to the priest as a gift by Eraldo Polato, then co-owner of the Verona Soccer Team. "Using that 800-cubic-centimeter, thirty-horsepower economy car with the four-speed stick shift next to the steering wheel and reclining seats, Fr. Renzo began driving up and down the neighborhood, going beyond the parish boundaries as well: summer camps, summer prayer and service projects, welcome centers, the Aosta Valley, the Dolomites, Rome and so on. . . . Finally the odometer reading was 300,000 kilometers." Even though the car was squeezed like a lemon and used to the limit of its capabilities, it never broke down on the road. . . .

Fr. Zocca, struck by the words of the new Pope about the marginalized, wrote to Francis to talk to him about his experience and to give him a gift: the white Renault 4. Several weeks later, "at 10:19 on August 10, to be precise", the pastor was in his rectory. His telephone rang,

and at the other end the priest from Verona heard someone say to him, "This is Pope Francis."

"I was unable to speak; it took my breath away. I did
not know what to say! How do you answer a Pope on the
telephone? At last I said: 'Praised be Jesus Christ', which
is always appropriate, I thought." The priest relates that
the conversation lasted for more than a half hour. "I told
him about my pastoral project among the marginalized,
and he was very interested. Then I confirmed my offer
to give him the Renault 4. 'Are you absolutely sure?' he
asked me. 'Do you really want to give it to me? Is it not
better to give it to the poor?' I replied that that car had
already done a great deal for the poor and that now it
should go to the Pope, and in my excitement I did not
notice that I had raised my voice. 'Do you have another
car?' Francis asked me. When I replied that I still had a
more recent car, the Pope was finally convinced and told
me: 'Then let us meet here at my place; wait while I get
my date-book.' I hear the rustling of a few pages, then:
'Well, I am free on September 5, 6, or 7, at 3:00, 4:00, or
5:00. When do you want to come?' I answered instinc-
tively: 'Wait until I get my date book', and I stood up
to get it. At a certain point, while I was already standing,
I realized that I was speaking on the telephone with the
Holy Father. I excused myself for the gaffe, he answered
by laughing, and we agreed on September 7 at 3:00 in the
afternoon."

The old economy car was entrusted to the care of Stefano the mechanic, who serviced it, waxed and polished
it, tuned up the engine and checked the pressure on the

tires. Then it was hitched to a tow truck and was off to Rome, followed by around a hundred pilgrims traveling by train in a Pullman car. For security reasons, only half of them were allowed to enter the Vatican to witness the moment when the car was presented to the Pope. But Fr. Renzo told Francis about the others waiting outside. The Pope said: "Then let's go!" "Four of us got into the car: I was at the wheel," Fr. Renzo recalls, "he was in the passenger seat, and Stefano the mechanic and my assistant Luigi were in the back. Stefano told me: 'Go slowly, we're in the Vatican!' The speedometer read thirty kilometers per hour [19 mph]. I cannot tell you how excited those fifty parishioners were to see the R4 arrive and the Holy Father get out.'"

〜

The Little Cardinal of
the Sisters in Buenos Aires

Jesus asks of us the joy of the feast. The joy of being
Christians.

Morning meditation in the chapel of the
Domus Sanctae Marthae, September 6, 2013

At the archbishop's chancery in Buenos Aires there
are nuns who are employed to look after the priests
and to cook for them. They have been there for many
years.

Bergoglio's successor, Archbishop Mario Aurelio Poli,
related that these sisters have several finches. During the
twenty years in which he ate lunch there, Bergoglio always gave them the bread crumbs.

Moreover someone gave a gift of two cardinals, with
red plumage. They are there in a cage, alongside the other
winged tenants, and sing all day. Now there are two cardinals, a goldfinch, a black-headed finch, and a nightingale.

Pope Francis called the chancery, and one of the older
sisters picked up the phone and asked, "Who is calling?"

Now if the party he is trying to reach does not answer the phone directly, he does not immediately reveal his identity, but instead says: "This is Jorge, I'm calling from abroad." And in fact he has presented himself in that way on various occasions. "When you receive a telephone call of that sort," Archbishop Poli said, "know that it is the Pope." The next time Bergoglio called, the elderly nun asked, "But who is this? The cardinal?" He replied, jokingly, "No, this is the nightingale!"

~

Consolation for Michael

Leave behind the self-interest that hardens your
heart, overcome the indifference that makes your
heart insensitive towards others, conquer your
deadly reasoning, and open yourself to dialogue
and reconciliation.

Vigil of Prayer for Peace, September 7, 2013

The mother of Michael, a little boy from Pinerolo in
Northwest Italy afflicted with muscular dystrophy,
was really not expecting it. Raffaele De Santis, president
of the Santa Monica Association, which treats muscular
dystrophy patients, had sent a message to the Vatican asking the Pontiff to receive the boy and his parents in an
audience. In reply he had received a letter saying that the
Pope's obligations did not allow private audiences. In an
e-mail De Sanctis wrote: "If things do not improve, there
is a chance that he will have to undergo a tracheotomy.
The boy is letting himself go, but if it is not possible
to meet you, he would like to receive a telephone call
from you." Michael needed encouragement to continue
his treatments and not to give up.

At 12:10 on September 13, in a first-floor apartment of

a housing project in Pinerolo, the telephone rang. Antonella, the boy's mother, answered. "Good morning, this is Pope Francis and I wanted to talk with Michael." Deeply moved, the woman held the receiver up to her son's ear. "It really was the Pope. He spoke to me calmly for about ten minutes", Michael told *La Stampa*. "Incredible: the Pope telephoning me."

"When Mom told me that the Pope was on the phone, I thought what anyone would think about receiving a phone call from an important person. I thought that it was a joke. I started to laugh: who could ever believe that the Pope would call you directly, without even being announced first by his secretary?"

"It was enough for me to hear his voice", Michael said. "It was identical to the one that I hear when he speaks on television. It was no joke. It really was the Pope asking for me on the telephone. How cool is that?! I did not even get emotional and I answered his questions honestly. I did not even get excited at the time."

"Francis told me that he would have liked to meet me, that I would have to go to Rome, that he wanted to see me in person, but that he had many obligations at the moment and so he decided to telephone me. Who knows if I will ever go to Rome; it takes so much money to travel by air."

After the telephone call, the boy started to laugh for so long that he had tears in his eyes. "It did not seem possible to me. Then my Mom immediately posted the news on my Facebook page, and a little later the telephone began to ring: friends calling, but also many journalists, to whom I always repeated the same story."

The telephone call from Francis was a great encouragement for Michael. "Now I am doing better. I am still excited, I feel like somebody important. At 6:00 this evening I am going to Mass and I want to tell the bishop and my pastor about this telephone call. Maybe he has never had the opportunity to speak with the Pope, but I have."

When the journalist from *La Stampa* asked him what he would do when he went back home after the Mass, the boy replied: "As always, I will start mixing techno music on the computer, then watch some television, but for sure before going to bed I will do what the Pope asked me to do: I will pray for him."

∽

"Your child? I will baptize him."

To follow Jesus means to share his merciful love for
every human being.

@Pontifex (on Twitter), September 12, 2013

One of the surprise telephone calls by Pope Francis
that has entered the public domain was particularly
moving. "That telephone call lasted only a few minutes,
but it changed my life", Anna Romano told the *Corriere
della Sera*, an Italian daily newspaper. "The Pope called me
and told me that I was very brave and strong for having
decided to keep my baby, even though the father aban-
doned me. And he promised to baptize him personally."

Anna is a thirty-five-year-old Roman woman, who
moved to Arezzo a few months ago, where she found
a job as a saleswoman in a jeweler's shop, after the business in the capital for which she worked was shuttered. In
late June, the woman had written a letter to Pope Francis,
and she had turned to him as though to a father, confiding
in him.

Anna had just discovered two things. First, she was
pregnant. Second, the father of her child was already married and had a child.

"He left me and told me that he had no intention of

taking care of the baby on the way. He even advised me to have an abortion. For a moment I thought of actually doing that, but now the mere idea gives me the shivers. But at that time I was so alone and unhappy." The woman had the idea of writing to Pope Francis. She decided, though, to continue the pregnancy with the support of her family. Then she left with her relatives for a short vacation and gave no more thought to the letter that she had sent to "His Holiness Francis, Vatican City".

On Tuesday, September 3, around four in the afternoon, her telephone rang: "I answered it and was speechless." Because the caller, according to the woman, was Pope Francis in person. "At first I thought it was a joke, but then he referred to the letter. And only my best friend and my parents knew the things that I had written to him." It was a short telephone call, but very intense emotionally. "He told me that he had read my letter, that we Christians must not let anything take hope away from us", Anna added. "When I told him that I wanted to baptize my child, but was afraid that it might not be possible because I am an unwed mother, and already divorced besides, he told me that if I could not find a spiritual father of my own for the baptism, he himself would consider administering the sacrament to my little one."

The woman now carries this promise in her heart: "I do not know whether the Pope will actually find the time to baptize my child, who will be born in early April and whom I want to name Francis, if it is a boy. But that phone call made me happy and gave me strength. And I tell my story because I would like to be an example for many women who feel estranged from the Church just because they chose the wrong man, are divorced, or because they chose men who are not even worthy to be fathers."

This example is along the lines of Bergoglio's pastoral approach when he was Archbishop of Buenos Aires. An approach suited to a "Church of the people" that "facilitates" the faith of individuals instead of "regulating" it. In 2009, when interviewed by Gianni Valente for the magazine *30Giorni* [*30Days*], he had recounted this incident:

> Just a few days ago I baptized seven children of a woman on her own, a poor widow, who works as a maid, and she had had them from two different men. I met her last year at the Feast of San Cayetano [Cajetan]. She had told me: "Father, I'm in mortal sin, I have seven children and I've never had them baptized." It had happened because she had no money to bring the godparents from a distance, or to pay for the party, because she always had to work. . . . I suggested that we meet to talk about it. We spoke on the phone, she came to see me, told me that she could never find all the godparents and get them together. . . . In the end I said: let's do everything with only two godparents, representing the others. They all came here, and after a little catechesis I baptized them in the chapel of the archbishop's chancery. After the ceremony we had a little refreshment. A soft drink and sandwiches. She told me: "Father, I can't believe it, you make me feel important. . . ." I replied, "But *Señora*, where do I come in? Jesus is the one who makes you important."

MARIAN
LITTLE FLOWERS

~

The First Outing Is for Mary

Mary, remind us that those who believe are never alone.

Lumen Fidei, 60

O n the evening of March 13, 2013, at the end of his first appearance on the central balcony of St. Peter's Basilica, the new Pope who had come "from the end of the earth" announced to the faithful that on the following morning he would go to the Basilica of St. Mary Major to ask Our Lady, who is venerated there in the ancient icon called *"Salus Populi Romani"* [Health of the Roman People], to protect Rome. He had done this while making with his hands the gesture of receiving and protecting. No sooner said than done. At eight o'clock the next morning, Francis arrived at the basilica, the most ancient church dedicated to the Blessed Virgin, and entered, carrying in his own hands a little vase of flowers, his homage to the *Madonna* who protects the Eternal City.

The *Salus Populi Romani* is dated between the seventh and the twelfth centuries. It is a copy of an icon according to tradition painted by St. Luke, of an image of Mary with the Infant Jesus that appeared miraculously in Lydda in a church built by the Apostles Peter and John. Preserved first in Byzantium, the story goes, the icon made its way to Rome by sea and was welcomed by Pope Gregory the Great on the banks of the Tiber.

Cardinal Cesare Baronio, a Church historian, wrote that Gregory was the one who brought the icon into the Basilica of St. Mary Major in 590, with a procession to implore the end of a very serious plague. On that occasion the Archangel Michael was seen above Hadrian's Tomb, placing his sword back into its scabbard. The plague ended and the Tomb acquired the name of Castel Sant'Angelo. The Jesuits gave their first missions in the presence of reproductions of that icon, which they greatly venerated.

Pope John Paul II had wanted a copy of this icon to be present at the World Youth Day 2000 in Rome. And starting with WYD 2005 in Cologne, the first one of Benedict XVI, the young people have always carried in procession a reproduction of the *Salus Populi Romani*.

In the first six months of his pontificate, Francis made five personal visits to the icon to pray before it. After the visit on the day after his election, the Pope returned on May 4 to recite the Rosary during the month dedicated to Our Lady. Then he stopped by on the day of the Feast of Corpus Christi, at the end of the procession that started from the Basilica of St. John Lateran. Then he appeared before the *Salus Populi Romani* on the day before he left for the WYD in Rio de Janeiro. On that occasion he intended to ask Our Lady "for her protection for the upcoming apostolic journey to Brazil, for the young people who will gather at the World Youth Day of Rio de Janeiro and for all the young people of the world".

"In front of the Marian image," Fr. Federico Lombardi explained, "the Pope spent a long time in silent prayer, for more than a half hour, then offered a floral homage and lit a candle that also bore the WYD logo."

Upon returning to Rome from Brazil, even before re-entering the Vatican, despite the fatigue due to the very intense week and the twelve-hour flight, Francis decided to appear once again at Mary's feet. From Ciampino Airport he went directly to St. Mary Major, where he thanked Our Lady for the completion of WYD and placed on the altar a beach ball and a sports jersey, a gift from the young people.

At the conclusion of the Rosary on May 4, 2013, the Pope had said:

Mary is the mother, and a mother worries above all about the health of her children, she knows how to care for them always with great and tender love. Our Lady guards our health. What does this mean: Our Lady guards our health? I think above all of three things: she helps us grow, to confront life, to be free. . . .

Mary's whole life is a hymn to life, a hymn of love to life: she generated Jesus in the flesh and accompanied the birth of the Church on Calvary and in the Upper Room. The *Salus Populi Romani* is the mother that gives us health in growth, she gives us health in facing and overcoming problems, she gives us the health to make us free to make definitive choices. The mother teaches us how to be fruitful, to be open to life and to always bear good fruit, joyful fruit, hopeful fruit, and never to lose hope, to give life to others, physical and spiritual life.

Mary, Untier of Knots

There is an urgent need, then, to see once again that faith is a light, for once the flame of faith dies out, all other lights begin to dim.

Lumen Fidei, 4

One of the devotions of Pope Francis is a little-known one that he himself, as Bishop of Buenos Aires, helped to spread in Argentina. We mean devotion to Mary, Untier of Knots.

In the Eighties, during his studies abroad in Germany, Father Bergoglio discovered this Bavarian devotional image that dates back to the 1600s, "Mary, Untier of Knots" (*Maria Knotenlöserin*), the work of the German painter Johann Melchior Schmidtner, which is currently preserved in a chapel of St. Peter's in Perlach, a Romanesque church staffed by the Jesuits in the heart of Augsburg, in Bavaria.

After returning to Argentina, the future Pope, struck by the profound significance of this devotion, began to spread it, and immediately he met with remarkable approval among simple believers. "Once he became Auxiliary Bishop of Buenos Aires," Stefania Falasca recalled, writing in *Avvenire*, "he worked to have a shrine dedicated to the image of Mary, Untier of Knots." A local artist made a reproduction of the picture and thus on December 8, 1996, in the Church of San José del Talar in Buenos Aires, "Our Lady, Untier of Knots" was enthroned in the presence of thousands of the Argentine faithful.

After becoming Archbishop, Bergoglio further strengthened the devotion, continuing to dedicate chapels in her honor and also making use of that particular image "as a personal calling card, when writing to people near and far". Those who see the image of "Our Lady, Untier of Knots" for the first time are surprised by the rather unusual representation of Mary that is found in it. Indeed, Our Lady is not depicted with the Child Jesus, but rather assumed into heaven, with her feet crushing the serpent's head and intent on untying with her hands the knots in a ribbon that is being handed to her by two angels.

Standing at attention at her side, one of the two angels holds out to Our Lady the ribbon, which is tangled with knots large and small. On the other side, the ribbon, now smooth and reflecting the light of divine mercy and salvation, glides through the hands of the second angel, who shows it with an eloquent expression to the believer whose prayers have been heard, whose knot has been untied by the intervention of Mary's hands.

"The painting, as an *ex voto*," Falasca explains, "was meant to evoke in a simple way the grace received by the person who commissioned it, restoring his marriage (a ribbon, indeed, according to the customs of the time, symbolized conjugal union). The iconographic image and Mary's gesture are nevertheless fraught with broader allegorical meanings that are underscored and suggested by

Bergoglio", who refers to the words of Irenaeus of Lyons in his work *Adversus haereses* [Against Heresies], as cited in the Dogmatic Constitution on the Church, *Lumen gentium*, 56. In that conciliar document we read: "The Father of mercies willed that the Incarnation should be preceded by assent on the part of the predestined mother, so that just as a woman had a share in bringing about death, so also a woman should contribute to life. . . ." Whereas Irenaeus wrote: "The knot of Eve's disobedience was untied by Mary's obedience: what the virgin Eve bound through her disbelief, Mary loosened by her faith."

Our Lady therefore was and is present in every age as the "untier of knots" of sin and evil. As Bergoglio explained many times, "We all have knots in our heart, failings, and we go through difficulties. Our good Father, who distributes grace to all his children, wants us to have confidence in her, and to entrust to her the knots of our misfortunes, the tangles of our miseries which prevent us from being united to God, so that she may smooth them and bring us close to her Son Jesus. This is the meaning of the image."

The Auxiliary Bishop of Madrid and Secretary General of the Spanish Bishops' Conference, Juan Antonio Martinez Camino, suggested praying to "Our Lady, Untier of Knots" for Pope Francis, that she might keep him and support him with her maternal care in the task that has been entrusted to him.

Here is an English translation of the "Prayer to Mary, Untier of Knots" printed in Spanish and distributed with the *imprimatur* of the then-Archbishop of Buenos Aires, Jorge Mario Bergoglio:

Mary, untier of knots, Holy Mary, full of the presence of God, during the days of your life you accepted with all humility the Father's will, and the Evil One was never able to entangle you with his deceits.

Already joined to your Son, you interceded for us in our difficulties, and with the utmost simplicity and patience you gave us an example of how to untangle the yarn of our life.

And by remaining forever Our Mother, you put in order and make clearer the ties that bind us to the Lord.

Holy Mary, Mother of God and our Mother, with a motherly heart you loosen the knots that shackle our life; we ask you to receive us in your hands and to free us from the knots and confusion with which our enemy torments us.

Through your grace, through your intercession, and by your example, deliver us from all evil, Our Lady, and untie the knots that keep us from being united with God, so that, free from all confusion and error, we may find Him in all things, set our hearts on Him, and be able to serve Him always in our brothers and sisters. *Amen.*

～

The Statuette Cradled Like a Child

God always saves the best for us. But he asks us to
let ourselves be surprised by his love, to accept his
surprises.

*Homily at the Shrine of Our Lady of the
Conception of Aparecida, July 24, 2013*

There is a moving image that went around the world
during Francis' journey to Brazil. On July 24 the
Pope wanted to make a pilgrimage to Aparecida, to the
most important Marian shrine in the country. It is said
that initially he intended to do so privately, but obviously
that was not possible. It was pouring rain on that day, and
many people were waiting for Francis outside, in the large
square in front of the shrine.

This was precisely where, in May 2007, the meeting
of all the bishops of Latin America took place, and then-
Cardinal Bergoglio had had a decisive role, as the one
responsible for composing the final document.

In the shrine, a little statue of the black Madonna is
venerated; the statuette, sixteen inches tall, was retrieved
in three pieces in October 1717 in the Paraiba River by
three fishermen. Tradition has it that it is black because
Our Lady wants to remain alongside the oppressed, and
that the fact that it was fished out of the water in pieces

recalled the shattered life of slavery. At the end of the Mass, Francis took the statuette and carried it with him onto the balcony of the shrine, where he was to greet the crowd that had not been able to find a place inside. The Pope walked through the nave holding the statue as though holding a child, almost cradling it.

This gesture once again testifies to his tenderness, his great Marian devotion and also his deep attachment to popular devotions.

And Francis referred precisely to this atmosphere of prayer of the simple faithful in his homily in Aparecida, recalling one particular and important element:

> There is something that I would like to say first of all. Six years ago the Fifth General Conference of the Bishops of Latin America and the Caribbean was held in this Shrine. Something beautiful took place here, which I witnessed at first hand. I saw how the Bishops—who were discussing the theme of encountering Christ, discipleship and mission—felt encouraged, supported and in some way inspired by the thousands of pilgrims who came here day after day to entrust their lives to Our Lady. That Conference was a great moment of the Church. It can truly be said that the Aparecida Document was born of this interplay between the labors of the Bishops and the simple faith of the pilgrims, under Mary's maternal protection. When the Church looks for Jesus, she always knocks at his Mother's door and asks: "Show us Jesus". It is from Mary that the Church learns true discipleship. That is why the Church always goes out on mission in the footsteps of Mary.
>
> Today, looking forward to the World Youth Day that

has brought me to Brazil, I too come to knock on the door of the house of Mary—who loved and raised Jesus —that she may help all of us, pastors of God's people, parents and educators, to pass on to our young people the values that can help them build a nation and a world which are more just, united and fraternal.

Francis then commented on the day's reading, which presents the encounter between the Woman and the dragon.

A woman—an image of Mary and the Church—is being pursued by a Dragon—the devil—who wants to devour her child. But the scene is not one of death but of life, because God intervenes and saves the child. How many difficulties are present in the life of every individual, among our people, in our communities; yet as great as these may seem, God never allows us to be overwhelmed by them.

In the face of those moments of discouragement we experience in life, in our efforts to evangelize or to embody our faith as parents within the family, I would like to say forcefully: Always know in your heart that God is by your side; he never abandons you! Let us never lose hope! Let us never allow it to die in our hearts! The "dragon", evil, is present in our history, but it does not have the upper hand. The one with the upper hand is God, and God is our hope!

Francis concluded his homily by recalling that "Christians are joyful, they are never gloomy. God is at our side. We have a Mother who always intercedes for the life of her children, for us."

Mary Opens the Gate of Paradise

If we are afraid, let us remember that our Mother is
with us, and like children who are a bit scared, let us
go to her.

Morning meditation in the chapel of the
Domus Sanctae Marthae, July 6, 2013

On August 15, 2013, before the Mass of the Assumption at Castel Gandolfo, Pope Francis paid a visit
to the Poor Clare nuns of the cloistered monastery in
Albano. Vatican Radio interviewed the Mother Abbess,
Maria Assunta Fuoco, and her assistant, Sr. Maria Concetta Sfregola. The latter recounted:

The Pope was calm, relaxed, as though he had nothing on his mind and nothing else to do. He spoke to
us—in a way that was quite striking for us—about
Mary, on that Solemnity of the Assumption. A consecrated woman is a little like Mary. He told us something charming, something beautiful that made everyone smile, him included: Mary is inside the gate of
Paradise; St. Peter does not always open the door when
sinners arrive, and then Mary suffers a little, but she remains there. And at night, when the gates of Paradise
are closed, when no one sees and no one hears, Mary

opens the gate of Paradise and invites them all to enter. There you have it! We saw again, in this, our mission, our vocation. This vocation to the contemplative life, in the cloister, today is not at all understood, but that does not matter! Why is it essential? What is the purpose of this life, of this vocation? I believe that it is precisely this. And today the Pope in a few words said it to us again. In silence, in the darkness, in the night, when no one sees, no one knows, no one hears, how many people go past monasteries of contemplative life and do not even know who is inside and why they are there! Look: in this silence, in this night our mission is carried out: being able to open the gates of Paradise so as to let all humanity enter, all the human beings, the brothers and sisters who perhaps have not even heard about, do not even know and maybe do not have the gift of faith. Like Mary to open that gate, to restore trust and hope. No one knows . . . but that does not matter to us. But God knows; Mary knows!

~

LITTLE FLOWERS
WITH A SMILE

~

The Pope Who Smiles

A sad bishop: how bad is that! So that my faith might not be sad, I came here to be filled with your contagious enthusiasm!

Greeting to the Young People,
Waterfront of Copacabana, July 25, 2013

M any witnesses who had been closely acquainted with Jorge Mario Bergoglio before his election agree that, when they saw him again afterward, they found him almost rejuvenated, with new energy and smiling more than ever. A statement of this sort was made, for example, by Fr. José Maria di Paola, nicknamed "Pepe", a pastor in the *"villas miserias"* [shanty-towns] of Buenos Aires, after a two-hour meeting with Francis.

A similar reaction was reported also by Mario Aurelio Poli, the archbishop that Bergoglio chose as his successor in the see of the Argentine capital. Archbishop Poli, after his most recent encounter with Francis, said: "Here he had a facial expression . . . that we call. . . . Have you ever seen boys misbehaving and then their mothers say: 'No joy for me?' And the way mothers say, 'No joy here?'"

"Well, that", the Archbishop of Buenos Aires continued, "is how we used to talk to the Pope when he was here. 'No joy here?' Always with a funereal expression. A face like that, always serious, but with a heart of gold. He would go to the 'shanty-towns'. In the shanty-towns there are two sacraments to celebrate . . . actually, there are three: the Eucharist, Confirmation and . . . the photo. You have to stay there, like the clown at McDonald's, and for an hour and a half all the families line up to have their photo taken. And one pastor had said to Bergoglio: 'If you come with that expression, you will ruin all our photos!' "

Now, though the Pope's face has changed; he smiles more. Archbishop Poli confirms this: "Now the Pope is all smiles! He smiles at everyone, and we tell him, 'Well? Back there, not even a grin, and here all smiles! Here there are smiles for the whole world.' And he lifts his chin and replies, 'It is the fruit of the Spirit.' "

During his long interview with the journalists on the flight from Rio de Janeiro to Rome, Francis, answering one question, spoke about his ministry as a bishop:

To do the work of a bishop is a wonderful thing; it is wonderful. The problem arises when someone seeks that work: this is not so good, this is not from the Lord. But when the Lord calls a priest to become a bishop, this is good. There is always the danger of thinking one-self a little superior to others, not like others, some-thing of a *prince*. There are dangers and sins, *no*? But the work of a bishop is wonderful: it is to help one's broth-ers and sisters to move forward. The bishop *ahead* of the faithful, to mark out the path; the bishop *in the midst* of the faithful, to foster communion; and the bishop *behind* the faithful, because the faithful can often sniff out the path. The bishop must be like that. You asked me whether I like it. Yes, I like being a bishop, I like it. In Buenos Aires I was very happy, very happy! I was happy, it's true. The Lord helped me in that. But as a priest I was happy, and as a bishop I was happy. In this sense I say: I like it!

These words seemed to give the impression that that "happiness" was connected only with the time of his episcopate in Argentina. One journalist shouted, "And as Pope?" Bergoglio went on: "Likewise, likewise! When the Lord puts you there, if you do what the Lord wants, you are happy. This is my feeling, eh? This is how I feel."

This is the secret of Francis' smile. Even though life in the Vatican notoriously imposes restrictions and as Bishop of Rome it is no longer possible to have all the freedom that is granted to the Bishop of Buenos Aires.

~

To Priests and Nuns He Says:
Do Not Be Bachelors and Spinsters

It's a bit sad when one comes across a priest without hope, . . . and it is very beautiful when one comes across a priest who is reaching the end of his life still filled with that hope, not with optimism, but with hope, and who is sowing hope.

*Morning Meditation in the chapel of the
Domus Sanctae Marthae, September 9, 2013*

According to Francis, even someone who has chosen celibacy must be "fruitful", generate children, even though not in the flesh. And that person must not appear to be a bachelor or a spinster. The Pope said this during his meeting with seminarians, novices, and young people discerning their vocations, whom he met in Paul VI Audience Hall on July 6, 2013.

Bergoglio, speaking impromptu, said:

Do not be afraid to show the joy of having answered the Lord's call, of having responded to his choice of love and of bearing witness to his Gospel in service to the Church. And joy, true joy, is contagious; it is infectious . . . it impels one forward. Instead when you

meet a seminarian who is excessively serious, too sad,
or a novice like this, you think: but something has gone
wrong here! The joy of the Lord is lacking, the joy
that prompts you to serve, the joy of the encounter
with Jesus which brings you to encounter others to
proclaim Jesus. This is missing! There is no holiness
in sadness, there isn't any! St. Teresa—there are many
Spaniards here and they know it well—said: "A saint
who is sad is a sad saint." It is not worth much. . . .
When you see a seminarian, a priest, a sister or a novice
with a long face, gloomy, who seems to have thrown a
soaking wet blanket over their life, one of those heavy
blankets . . . which pulls one down. . . . Something
has gone wrong!

But please: never any sisters, never any priests with
faces like "chilis pickled in vinegar"—never! The joy
that comes from Jesus. Think about this: when a priest
—I say a priest, but also a seminarian—when a priest
or a sister lacks joy, when he or she is sad, you might
think: "but this is a psychological problem, isn't it?"
. . . It might happen: some, poor things, fall sick. However in general it is not a psychological problem. Is it a
problem of dissatisfaction?

Well, yes! But what is at the heart of this lack of
joy? It is a matter of celibacy. I will explain to you.
You, seminarians, sisters, consecrate your love to Jesus,
a great love. Your heart is for Jesus and this leads us to
make the vow of chastity, the vow of celibacy. However the vow of chastity and the vow of celibacy do not
end at the moment the vow is taken, they endure. . . .
A journey that matures, that develops toward pastoral
fatherhood, towards pastoral motherhood, and when a

priest is not a father to his community, when a sister is not a mother to all those with whom she works, he or she becomes sad. This is the problem. For this reason I say to you: the root of sadness in pastoral life is precisely in the absence of fatherhood or motherhood that comes from living this consecration unsatisfactorily, which instead should lead us to fertility. It is impossible to imagine a priest or a sister who is not fertile: this is not Catholic! This is not Catholic! This is the beauty of consecration: it is joy, joy. . . .

And he concludes:

And on we go, with joy, with consistency, always with the courage to tell the truth, the courage to step out of ourselves to meet Jesus in prayer and to step out of ourselves to encounter others and give the Gospel to them. With pastoral fruitfulness! Please do not be "spinsters" and "bachelors".

~

The Nuns "let loose" and the Skipped Siesta

Never be men and women of sadness.

Homily on Palm Sunday,
March 24, 2013

F rancis' alarm clock, in room 201 of the Casa Santa Marta, rings at a little after four, while everything is still immersed in darkness. Rising so early makes it necessary to take a siesta after the midday meal, the rest that the Argentine President Juan Domingo Perón once described as "an almost liturgical obligation" that allowed him to have "two mornings" every day. The timetables for the Pope did not change during his journey to Rio de Janeiro in July 2013. In fact, because of the change of time zone, he rose even earlier than usual. Francis devoted these extra hours during the night and day to prayer and meditation on the readings.

But on July 25, the day dedicated to visiting the shrine of Our Lady of Aparecida, the most important Marian shrine in Brazil, Pope Francis had to give up his siesta. Because of duties of state? No. An impromptu summit meeting with the cardinals to discuss the future of the

Church? Not that, either. The ones who prevented him with their enthusiasm and their insistence from taking his salutary afternoon nap were some cloistered nuns. The head of the Press Office of the Holy See, Fr. Federico Lombardi, related this to the journalists with some amusement. The nuns had gone to meet the Pope at the seminary in Aparecida, where Bergoglio stayed after celebrating the morning Mass. "You might have expected that the sisters would be calm and silent," Fr. Lombardi commented ironically, "but instead, even though they were outdoors in the courtyard of the seminary and it was raining, they really let loose in welcoming the Pontiff."

That is exactly how he put it: they "let loose". . . .

"Not only that," Lombardi went on to say, "the sisters demanded that each one of them should have a photo with the Pontiff and his autograph, because they maintained that they were all equal in his eyes. And therefore Francis remained with him the whole time that was allotted for his rest. Consequently, a later meeting with the police—all of them young men from whom you might have expected a more lively response than from the sisters —turned out to be much more orderly and calm."

Patient, smiling, caught up too in the enthusiasm that carried away the cloistered nuns, Bergoglio let himself be photographed with each one of them, and to each one he gave his autograph. To get a bit of rest he had to wait for the more orderly audience with the policemen.

~

"I need a community"

Sometimes it is possible to live without knowing our neighbors: this is not Christian.

> @Pontifex (on Twitter),
> September 14, 2013

W hy did Pope Francis decide to become a Jesuit? He explains it as follows in his interview with the editor of *La Civiltà Cattolica*, Fr. Antonio Spadaro.

> I wanted something more. But I did not know what. I entered the diocesan seminary. I liked the Dominicans and I had Dominican friends. But then I chose the Society of Jesus, which I knew well because the seminary was entrusted to the Jesuits. Three things in particular struck me about the Society: the missionary spirit, community, and discipline. And this is strange, because I am a really, really undisciplined person. But their discipline, the way they manage their time—these things struck me so much.
>
> And then a thing that is really important for me: community. I was always looking for a community. I did not see myself as a priest on my own. I need a community. And you can tell this by the fact that I am here in Santa Marta. At the time of the conclave I lived

in Room 207. (The rooms were assigned by drawing lots.) This room where we are now was a guest room. I chose to live here, in Room 201, because when I took possession of the papal apartment, inside myself I distinctly heard a "no". The papal apartment in the Apostolic Palace is not luxurious. It is old, tastefully decorated, and large, but not luxurious. But in the end it is like an inverted funnel. It is big and spacious, but the entrance is really tight. People can come only in dribs and drabs, and I cannot live without people. I need to live my life with others.

〰

"Maté, better for the digestion than tea or coffee"

Faith is revolutionary and today I ask you: are you open to entering into this revolutionary wave of faith?

Homily, Waterfront of Copacabana,
Rio de Janeiro, July 25, 2013

S igo tomando el maté. . . ," "I continue to drink maté." This is what Pope Francis wrote in a letter replying to the President of Argentina, Cristina Kirchner, who had sent Bergoglio a congratulatory message for the Feast of Ss. Peter and Paul, the patron saints of Rome.

"I continue to drink maté", reads the letter, which was made public by President Kirchner, "it is always better for the digestion than tea or coffee." This is the name for the infusion prepared with the leaves of the herb *maté*, a South American shrub. Following the same process as tea leaves, the herb maté is dried, cut, and pulverized. Traditionally people drink this infusion hot, with a special container and a sort of metal straw.

The tradition of drinking maté was adopted by the Spanish colonists from the Guarani Indians. In the period of the Jesuit reductions [settlements] in the Royal

Province of Guayra (today the State of Paraná, Brazil) in the sixteenth century, the Spanish soldiers, who were accustomed to tea, took this herb that was used by the indigenous people and added to it the metal straw, called a *bombilla*, and the hot water. The natives, on the other hand, used cold water to make maté. With the passage of time it was adopted as the traditional beverage in Argentina, Paraguay, Uruguay, Chile, and the Southern Region of Brazil and all along the Andes *cordillera* [mountain range].

In countries like Argentina, including its capital, Buenos Aires, drinking maté is a daily ritual in almost all families and, in some cases, even in offices, where it is very common to see professionals working in front of their computers with a cup of maté.

Since he was elected, Francis has already received several glasses and *bombillas* with which to drink maté. The first one was given to him by a journalist three days after the election. But certainly the oddest incident is still the one that took place during World Youth Day in Rio de Janeiro. One evening, while Francis, on board the popemobile, was making his way at a snail's pace along the beach of Copacabana, being greeted enthusiastically by thousands of young people, one of them came up to him holding in his hand a maté glass of considerable dimensions, with a *bombilla* to match, and offered it to the Pope. Francis took it in his hands for a moment and sipped the beverage, under the anxious scrutiny of his security detail.

LITTLE FLOWERS
OF COURAGE

~

"I would rather they kill me"

Faith is no refuge for the fainthearted, but something which enhances our lives. It makes us aware of a magnificent calling, the vocation of love.

Lumen Fidei, 53

I would rather they kill me than one of you. . . ." So said then-Cardinal Jorge Mario Bergoglio in response to the news about the death threats received by Fr. José María di Paola, "Padre Pepe", a parish priest in one of the *villas miserias*, the shanty-towns of Buenos Aires. "These words", the Argentine priest explains, "express better than any others the bishop's close, paternal relationship with his priests."

The first threats against the parish priest of Our Lady of Caacupó in Villa 21-24 of the Barracas district of Buenos Aires were made in the spring of 2009. Fr. Pepe and the other priests whom Bergoglio had sent to the *villas miserias* were working to rehabilitate the many young drug addicts. New and even more serious threats were made by the drug dealers in December 2010, and at that point the future Pope decided to take the priest out of harm's way and send him to another diocese in the northern part of the country. Today Fr. Pepe has returned to pastoral work in another *villa* and has resumed his priestly ministry in the shanty-towns.

In an interview with *30Giorni* after the initial threats, Bergoglio, speaking about his *cura villeros* (priests in the slums), Bergoglio said:

> They work. They don't attack anyone. I was the one who said that drugs are dangerous, not just in the *favelas* but throughout the city. . . . I told the parents: watch what your children are doing, look after them, because drugs show up everywhere, even at entrances of the schools. They, the priests in the *villas*, also work to prevent drug addiction and help reintegrate drug addicts back into society. A month ago, they had drafted a constructive proposal regarding the alarming growth in drug trafficking. Villa 21 recently opened three rehab centers for young drug addicts. Obviously the drug dealers didn't like this. It must have annoyed someone.

Fr. Pepe has now revealed some of the conversation that he had then with his archbishop. "They threatened me on Monday, on Tuesday I went to Bergoglio. I told him that this was a serious threat. His first reaction was to say to me: 'I would rather they kill me than one of you.'"

∽

Eusebio, the Guardian Angel of Nicolás and of the Pope

Mercy . . . is the Lord's most powerful message.

Homily, March 17, 2013

O n October 4, 2013, Pope Francis visited Assisi, the city of the saintly *Poverello* whose name he decided to take—the first pope in history to do so. His first appointment was the most moving. Bergoglio greeted, embraced, and kissed one by one the seriously disabled babies and children who are cared for at the Seraphic Institute. "My visit is above all a pilgrimage of love", he had written in the speech that he then did not give, preferring to speak a few words impromptu.

Unfortunately, society has been polluted by the culture of "waste", which is opposed to the culture of acceptance. And the victims of this culture of waste are precisely persons who are the weakest, the most fragile. In this home, however, I see a culture of acceptance in action. Of course, not everything can be perfect here either, but you are working together for a dignified life for those people in grave difficulty. Thank you for this sign of love that you offer us: this is a sign of true citizenship, human and Christian! Put the most disadvantaged people at the center of social and political attention! At times instead families find themselves alone in taking care of them. What should we do? In this place real love can be seen. I say to everyone: let us multiply our work in the culture of acceptance, works primarily enlivened by a deep Christian love, love for the Crucified Christ, for the flesh of Christ, works which join together professionalism—skilled work properly compensated—with volunteer work, a precious treasure.

Serving with love and tenderness those who are in great need helps us to grow in humanity because they are true resources of humanity. St. Francis was a rich young man, he had ideals of glory, but Jesus, in the person of a leper, spoke to him in silence and he changed him, he made him understand what truly matters in life: not wealth, or power or weapons, or earthly glory, but humility, mercy and forgiveness.

Then Francis decided to share with everyone the text of a letter.

Here, dear brothers and sisters, I want to read you something personal, one of the most beautiful letters I have received, a gift of love from Jesus. Nicolás, a sixteen-year-old boy, disabled at birth, who lives in Buenos Aires, wrote it to me. I will read it to you:

"Dear Francis, my name is Nicolás and I am sixteen years old; since I cannot write you (because I can neither write nor walk), I asked my parents to do it for me, because they are the people who know me best. I want to tell you that when I was six years old, in my school which is called Aedin, Fr. Pablo gave me First Communion, and this year in November I will receive Confirmation, something that gives me great joy. Every night, since you asked me, I ask my Guardian Angel, whose name is Eusebio and who has a lot of patience, to guard you and help you. You can be sure that he does it very well because he takes care of me and stays with me every day!! Ah! And when I am not tired . . . he comes to play with me!! I would very much like to come and see you and to receive your blessing and a kiss: only this!! I send you many greetings and continue to ask Eusebio to take care of you and to give you strength. Kisses. —NICO"

In this letter, in the heart of this boy, there is beauty, love, and the poetry of God. God who reveals himself to those who have a simple heart, to the little ones, to the humble and to those who we often consider to be last, even you, dear friends. That boy when he cannot fall asleep plays with his guardian angel; it is God who comes down to play with him.

The bishop asked that in the chapel of this Institute there be permanent eucharistic adoration: Jesus himself whom we adore in the sacrament and whom we meet in the most fragile of brothers, from whom we learn that God loves us with simplicity of heart without barriers or complications.

Security and "Madness"

The restlessness of love is always an incentive to go towards the other, without waiting for the other to manifest his need.

Message to the Augustinians,
August 29, 2013

By now it is common knowledge that, for Jorge Mario Bergoglio, the geographical peripheries and the margins of life are the real "center", the place to go to. The priests in the *favelas* know this very well—the ones whom the Archbishop of Buenos Aires sent to the *villas miserias*, the shanty-towns of the Argentine capital. But Bergoglio never limited himself merely to assigning priests from one place to another, while remaining seated in the chancery offices: he always accompanied them, helping and assisting them, inquiring about their needs and problems. And he always traveled alone, without escort or companions or any special precautions for his safety.

So reports Fr. José María di Paola, known to everyone as *"Padre Pepe"*, who for many years has done pastoral work in the *villas miserias*, especially in trying to free young people from drugs. "Bergoglio often came to visit us here," the priest tells us, and he always felt at ease and calm in the midst of the poor. Sometimes he arrived unexpectedly, without any announcement, without warning us first. One thing that he liked very much was to participate in the patronal feast days, to be with the people, to go into their houses, to speak with them, to share a bit of food. Sometimes I worried: I feared that when he arrived they might not recognize him and might attack him to rob him. For this reason I asked him always to tell us first; that way we could come to pick him up and accompany him. But his response was: "If I enter one of the *villas* I must do so like any other person and I have to meet with the same fate as any other inhabitant!"

Nothing ever happened to him during those visits to places that are considered highly unsuitable, where he wanted the Church to be present on the ground.

Against this backdrop one can understand better why Pope Francis, having arrived in the Vatican, never wanted security requirements to distance him from the people. This has been true not only in Rome, but also during his travels, as was evident during his visit to Brazil on the occasion of World Youth Day. On the first day, upon his arrival in Rio de Janeiro, Francis' automobile—the smallest of the papal procession, a Brazilian-made Fiat Idea with license plate "scv 1" ["Vatican City State 1"], got stuck in the middle of a street because of a routing error, with the enthusiastic crowd pressing in on every side to greet the Pope. During those days in Rio, the Pope cruised the length of the Copacabana beach four times in an open white jeep without bulletproof windows, so as to be able to lean out constantly, touch hands, receive tokens of respect and greet the children. The crowd of young people at WYD took to throwing toward the Pope caps, scarves, letters, flags, and rosaries, which by the end of the trip literally filled the popemobile. And during one drive the Pope also sipped a bit of maté—the herbal tea that is very common in Argentina—that was offered to him by some of the young people.

The Vatican police, the "guardian angels" assigned to keep Francis safe, had to get used to this new style. Some time before the journey, the Pope personally went to the Vatican parking lot to select from the fleet of vehicles the jeep to be driven through the streets of Rio de Janeiro. He did not want the popemobile that is always used on these sorts of journeys: the one that is enclosed and equipped with thick, bulletproof windows.

Before departing for Rome, in an interview with the Brazilian television network Globo, Francis explained:

> I am not afraid. I am reckless, but not afraid. I know that no one dies during Evening Prayer. When it happens, it will be as God wills. But, before the trip, I went to see the popemobile that was supposed to be sent to Brazil. It was all enclosed, with thick glass. If we want to be with the people we love, our friends, we want to communicate, not pay a visit in a glass house. No. I would not have been able to come here to see this big-hearted people while shut up in a glass box.

"And when I am in an automobile on the street," the Pope added,

I open the window, so as to be able to stretch out my hand and greet the people. I mean to say: it's all or nothing. Either we do the trip as it should be done, or we don't do it. Communication by half measures is no good. I am grateful—and on this point I must be very clear—for the Vatican security, for the way in which they prepared this visit, with the attentive care that they have always taken. And I also thank the Brazilian security. Very much indeed. Because here they take care of me, to prevent anything unpleasant from happening. Something could happen, someone might hit me . . . it could occur. All the security forces worked very well. Nevertheless, they know my lack of discipline in this sense. But not because I am acting like an undisciplined child. No. But rather because I came to visit these persons and I want to touch them.

On the airplane returning from Rio de Janeiro to Rome on the evening of July 28, Pope Bergoglio returned to the topic of security with similar remarks. He said:

Security here, security there; there wasn't a single accident in the whole of Rio de Janeiro during these days, and everything was spontaneous. With less security, I could have been with the people, I could have embraced them, greeted them, without armored cars . . . there is security in trusting a people. It is true that there is always the danger of some mad person . . . the danger that some mad person will do something, but then there is the Lord! But to make an armed space between the bishop and the people is madness, and I prefer the other madness: standing out in the open! . . . Closeness is good for us all.

Living on the Frontier
and Being Bold

When a young person says to me: "These are difficult times Father, we cannot do anything!" Well! I
send him or her to a psychiatrist! . . . It's impossible
to understand a young person who does not want to
do something great or bet on great ideals.

Address to young people,
August 28, 2013

T here is always the lurking danger of living in a laboratory." Pope Francis said this in his interview with
the editor of *La Civiltà Cattolica*, Antonio Spadaro. [The
interview was reprinted in English in *America* magazine.]
Francis is anxious to emphasize that the Christian faith
is not a test tube or a set of abstract norms. He went on
to explain:

> Ours is not a "lab faith", but a "journey faith", a his-
> torical faith. God has revealed himself as history, not as
> a compendium of abstract truths. I am afraid of labora-
> tories because in the laboratory you take the problems
> and then you bring them home to tame them, to paint
> them artificially, out of their context. You cannot bring
> home the frontier, but you have to live on the border
> and be audacious.

When asked to give some examples based on his personal experience, Pope Francis replied:

> When it comes to social issues, it is one thing to have a meeting to study the problem of drugs in a slum neighborhood and quite another thing to go there, live there, and understand the problem from the inside and study it. . . . One cannot speak of poverty if one does not experience poverty, with a direct connection to the places in which there is poverty.

Then Bergoglio referred to an illness that he almost died of, which kept him for a long time in the hospital when he was twenty-one years old. He remarked:

> The frontiers are many. Let us think of the religious sisters living in hospitals. They live on the frontier. I am alive because of one of them. When I went through my lung disease at the hospital, the doctor gave me penicillin and streptomycin in certain doses. The sister who was on duty tripled my doses because she was daringly astute; she knew what to do because she was with ill people all day. The doctor, who really was a good one, lived in his laboratory; the sister lived on the frontier and was in dialogue with it every day. Domesticating the frontier means just talking from a remote location, locking yourself up in a laboratory. Laboratories are useful, but reflection for us must always start from experience.

This is an extremely personal example of what it means to reflect in a laboratory and to reflect based on experience.

"What is needed is courageous prayer"

Faith is not a decorative or ornamental element; living faith does not mean decorating life with a little religion, as if it were a cake and we were decorating it with frosting.

Angelus, August 18, 2013

Miracles? They still happen today. Francis said this during his homily at the Mass he celebrated on May 20, 2013 in the chapel of the Domus Sanctae Marthae. But in order to make sure that the Lord works them, what is needed is courageous prayer, prayer that involves us personally and commits our whole life, so as to overcome disbelief.

The Pope commented on a passage from the Gospel of Mark that speaks about a boy possessed by an evil spirit, a passage in which Jesus laments unbelief. "This is not the first time", Francis said, "that Jesus laments unbelief: 'O faithless generation!' How many times he said this; and he suffered much because of this unbelief in his words, his message. They wished him well; the crowd went to greet him. They wished him well but up to a certain point. They did not risk too much in their belief with regard to him. They took no risks. And Jesus suffered as a result, didn't he? What he says today is intense: 'O faithless generation, how long am I to be with you? How long am I to bear with you?'"

The Pope repeated the question of the disciples of Jesus who had not succeeded in driving the evil spirit out of the boy: "Why could we not cast it out? This kind of demon, Jesus says, cannot be driven out by anything but prayer". The father of the possessed boy said: "Lord I believe, help my unbelief." His prayer, Francis explained, was "a strong prayer; and that strong and humble prayer moves Jesus to work the miracle. A prayer that calls for an extraordinary action must be a prayer that involves all of us, as though our very life depends on it. In prayer, you have to lay yourself on the line [*mettere la carne al fuoco*]."

The Pope related an incident that had taken place in Argentina: "I recall something that happened three years ago in the Shrine of Luján." A six-year-old girl had become seriously ill, but the doctors could not find a cure. Her condition kept getting worse, until finally, one evening, the doctors said that there was nothing left to do and that she had only a few hours to live.

"The father, who was an electrician, a man of faith," the Pope said, "became like a madman. And driven by that madness he took the bus and went to the Shrine of Luján, two and a half hours by bus, seventy kilometers [43 miles] away. He arrived at nine in the evening and found everything closed. And he began to pray with his hands gripping the iron gate. He prayed and wept. He remained that way the whole night. That man was wrestling with God. He was really wrestling with God for the healing of his little girl. Then at six in the morning he went to the terminal and took the bus. He arrived at the hospital at nine, more or less. He found his wife in tears, and he thought the worst: What happened? I don't understand. What happened? His wife replied: The doctors came and told me that the fever has disappeared, she is breathing well, there is nothing wrong. . . . They are going to keep her there for another two days. But they do not know what happened. . . ."

"And this", the Pope concluded, "still happens."

Miracles happen. But they need prayer! A courageous prayer, that struggles for that miracle. Not like those prayers of courtesy: Ah, I will pray for you! Followed by one Our Father, a Hail Mary, and then I forget. No! It takes a brave prayer like that of Abraham who was struggling with the Lord to save the city, like that of Moses who prayed, his hands held high, and he grew weary praying to the Lord; like the prayer of so many people who have faith and pray with faith.

Prayer works miracles, "but we must believe it."

I think that we can say a beautiful prayer, not a polite prayer, but a prayer from the heart, and tell him today throughout the whole day: Lord, I believe! Help my unbelief. We all have some unbelief in our heart. Let us say to the Lord: I believe, I believe! You can do it! Help my unbelief. And when we they ask us to pray for the many people who suffer in wars, as refugees, in all these tragedies let us pray, but with the heart, and let us say: Lord, I am failing. I believe, Lord. But help my unbelief.

LITTLE FLOWERS
OF SHARING

~

The Poor "share their heart"

Consumerism has induced us to be accustomed to
excess and to the daily waste of food.

General Audience, June 5, 2013

B y now it is well known that Archbishop Jorge Mario
Bergoglio often visited the *villas miserias*, the shanty-
towns of Buenos Aires. And that he liked to share meals
with the poor. The journalist Evangelina Himitian recorded the testimony of one inhabitant of the *villas*, Darío
Giménez.

"From the first time that he saw him on the 70 bus that
brought him to the Villa 21-24 of Barracas, Darío understood that Bergoglio was one of them. A common man."
Giménez is forty-three years old and works in a carpet
factory. He is the father of two children, ages eight and
six. "One of the most precious things that I cherish in
my heart is knowing that he baptized my daughter María
José. And I'm not just saying that now that he has become
Pope: I have always said it."

The man had met the future Pope through Fr. José
Maria di Paola, "Father Pepe", thanks to whom he had
converted to Christianity fourteen years previously. "Today", Evangelina Himitian wrote in her biography of

Francis, "he is a diligent coworker in the Church of Our Lady of Caacupé."

"Bergoglio is such a humble man," Darío Giménez explains, "that he always makes you feel at ease. The last time he came here to our house we invited him to dinner and he stayed to eat with us. We had not prepared anything elaborate, just a bit of pasta in broth, nothing else. I will never forget his words. Suddenly he looked me in the eyes and told me, 'I like to sit down at the table of the poor, because they serve food and share their heart. On the other hand, sometimes those who have more share only their food. . . .' He made me feel so good!" Darío recalls.

In October 2012, speaking at a meeting of Evangelical Christians and Catholics, during which the main speaker had been the preacher of the Papal Household, Fr. Raniero Cantalamessa, Bergoglio had said:

> Jesus spent much of his time on the road and today still continues to stand in our midst. The people do not miss the opportunity to stand by him. To touch him, to press in on him, to learn from him. I do not fear those who fight Jesus, because those individuals have already lost. I am more afraid of distracted, slumbering Christians who do not see Christ passing by. We have lost two things: the capacity to be surprised by our Lord's words, because we are bombarded by news stories that put the Good News in second place, and tenderness. Jesus came close to all human wounds and cured them. We must recover these two characteristics and not get used to seeing the sick or the hungry without being surprised or without feeling tenderness.

The Tragedy of Unemployment

We must be shocked at the injustice that not all
human beings have food and work.

Speech in Buenos Aires, August 2012

On September 22, 2013, Pope Francis visited Cagliari and celebrated Mass in the shrine of Our Lady of Bonaria, the patroness of Sardinia. It is because of this devotion and a group of Sardinian mariners that the Argentine capital is called Buenos Aires, *"Bon-aria,* good air".

The first meeting that the Pope had as soon as he had arrived on the island was his meeting with workers. Unemployment is a wound that is bringing Sardinia to its knees. Francis arrived at the city square, the *Largo Carlo Felice,* and found himself facing a crowd of laborers, unemployed men, and contractors who are seeking to address the crisis. He had prepared a speech, but when he looked into their eyes he preferred to speak off the cuff. To speak from the heart. And he began by recounting a familiar experience.

With this meeting I want above all to express my closeness to you, especially to the situations of suffering: to the many young people out of work, to people on

163

unemployment benefits, or on a temporary basis, to business and tradespeople who find it hard to keep going. I am very familiar with this situation because of my experience in Argentina. I myself was spared it but my family wasn't. My father went to Argentina as a young man full of illusions "of making it in America". And he suffered in the dreadful recession of the 1930s. They lost everything! There was no work! And in my childhood I heard talk of this period at home. . . . I never saw it, I had not yet been born, but I heard about this suffering at home, I heard talk of it. I know it well!

However, I must say to you: "Courage!" Nevertheless I am also aware that for own my part I must do everything to ensure that this term "courage" is not a beautiful word spoken in passing! May it not be merely the smile of a courteous employee, a Church employee who comes and says "be brave!" No! I don't want this! I want courage to come from within me and to impel me to do everything as a pastor, as a man. We must all face this challenge with solidarity, among you—also among us—we must all face with solidarity and intelligence this historic struggle.

This is the second city in Italy that I have visited. It is curious: both of them, the first one and this one, are on islands. In the first I saw the suffering of so many people on a quest, risking their life, their dignity, their livelihood, their health: the world of refugees. And I saw the response of that city which—as an island—did not want to isolate itself and receives them, makes them its own. It gives us an example of hospitality: suffering meets with a positive response. In this second city, an island that I am visiting, here too I find suffering. Suffering which, as one of you has said, "weakens you and ends by robbing you of hope". It is a form of suffering, the shortage of work, that leads you—excuse me if I am coming over a little strong, but I am telling the truth—to feel that you are deprived of dignity! Where there is no work there is no dignity! And this is not only a problem in Sardinia—but it is serious here!—it is not only a problem in Italy or in certain European countries, it is the result of a global decision, of an economic system which leads to this tragedy; an economic system centered on an idol called "money".

The Pope warned his listeners:

God did not want an idol to be at the center of the world but man, men and women who would keep the world going with their work. Yet now, in this system devoid of ethics, at the center there is an idol and the world has become an idolater of this "god-money". Money is in command! Money lays down the law! It orders all these things that are useful to it, this idol. . . .

Francis continued:

It is hard to have dignity without work. This is your difficulty here. This is the prayer you were crying out from this place: "work", "work", "work". It is a necessary prayer. Work means dignity, work means taking food home, work means loving! To defend this idolatrous economic system the "culture of waste" has become established; grandparents are thrown away and young people are thrown away. And we must say "no" to this "culture of waste." We must say: "We want a just system! A system that enables everyone to get on". We must say: "We don't want this globalized economic system which does us so much harm!" Men and women must be at the center, as God desires, and not money! . . .

I preferred to tell you what welled up from my heart, as I look at you now! You know, it is easy to say "Don't lose hope." But to all, to you all, those who have work and those who don't, I say: "Do not let yourselves be robbed of hope!" Perhaps hope is like embers under the ashes; let us help each other with solidarity, blowing on the ashes to rekindle the flame. But hope carries us onward. That is not optimism, it is something else. However hope does not belong to any one person, we all create hope! We must sustain hope in everyone, among all of you and among all of us who are far away. Hope is both yours and ours. It is something that belongs to everyone! This is why I am saying to you: "Do not let yourselves be robbed of hope!" But let us be cunning, for the Lord tells us that idols are more clever than we are. The Lord asks us to have the wisdom of serpents and the innocence of doves. Let us acquire this cunning and call things by their proper name. At this time, in our economic system, in our proposed globalized system of life there is an idol at the center and this is unacceptable! Let us all fight so that there may be men and women, families, all of us at the center— at least of our own life—so that hope can make headway. . . . . "Do not let yourselves be robbed of hope!"

The Pope concluded with a prayer, improvising a petition to the Lord.

I would now like to finish by praying with all of you in silence, in silence, praying with all of you. I shall say to you whatever wells up in my heart and please pray with me in silence:

Lord God look down upon us! Look at this city, this island. Look upon our families.

Lord, you were not without a job, you were a carpenter, you were happy.

Lord, we have no work.

The idols want to rob us of our dignity. The unjust systems want to rob us of hope.

Lord, do not leave us on our own. Help us to help each other; so that we forget our selfishness a little and feel in our heart the "we", the we of a people who want to keep on going.

Lord Jesus, you were never out of work, give us work and teach us to fight for work and bless us all. In the name of the Father, of the Son, and of the Holy Spirit.

Thank you very much and pray for me!

~

Men and Bricks

We must not be afraid of solidarity; rather let us
make all we have and are available to God.

@Pontifex (on Twitter), June 11, 2013

I n one week Pope Francis recalled three times this "midrash", a tale from the rabbinical tradition. He recalled
it to make us understand how little human life is valued
today, the life of the poor and the weak.

During the Vigil of Pentecost on May 18, 2013, Bergoglio said:

> There is one problem that can afflict Christians: the
> spirit of the world, the worldly spirit, spiritual world-
> liness. This leads to self-sufficiency, to living by the
> spirit of the world rather than by the spirit of Jesus. . . .
> How should we live in order to address this crisis that
> affects public ethics, the model of development and
> politics? Since this is a crisis of man, a crisis that de-
> stroys man, it is a crisis that strips man of ethics. In
> public life, in politics, if there is no ethics, an ethics of
> reference, everything is possible and everything can be
> done. We see, moreover, whenever we read the news-
> papers, that the lack of ethics in public life does great
> harm to the whole of humanity.

Francis continued:

I would like to tell you a story. I have already told it twice this week, but I will tell it a third time to you. It is taken from a biblical *midrash* by a twelfth-century rabbi. He tells the tale of the building of the Tower of Babel and he says that, in order to build the Tower of Babel, bricks had to be made. What does this mean? Going out and mixing the mud, fetching straw, doing everything . . . then the kiln. And when the brick was made it had to be hoisted for the construction of the Tower of Babel. Every brick was a treasure because of all the work required to make it. Whenever a brick fell, it was a national tragedy and the guilty workman was punished, a brick was so precious that if it fell it was a dramatic event. Yet if a workman fell, nothing happened, that was something else. This happens today: if the investments in the banks fall slightly . . . a tragedy . . . what can be done? But if people die of hunger, if they have nothing to eat, if they have poor health, it does not matter! This is our crisis today! And the witness of a poor Church for the poor goes against this mentality.

〜

Almsgiving Is
"touching the flesh of Christ"

Do not be afraid to go and to bring Christ into
every area of life, to the fringes of society, even to
those who seem farthest away, most indifferent.

Waterfront of Copacabana,
Rio de Janeiro, July 28, 2013

He had said so on several occasions as Archbishop of
Buenos Aires and repeated it during a ceremony
that was broadcast worldwide from St. Peter's Square on
the evening of Saturday, May 18, during the vigil of Pentecost, in which the ecclesial movements and associations
participated. Christians must "meet everyone" without
"losing sight" of their own position. They must step outside themselves and go toward the poor.

Today—it sickens the heart to say so—the discovery
of a tramp who has died of the cold is not news. Today what counts as news is, maybe, a scandal. A scandal: ah, that is news! Today, the thought that a great
many children do not have food to eat is not news. This
is serious, this is serious! We cannot put up with this!
Yet that is how things are. We cannot become starched

Christians, those over-educated Christians who speak
of theological matters as they calmly sip their tea. No!
We must become courageous Christians and go in
search of the people who are the very flesh of Christ,
those who are the flesh of Christ!

Then Francis related what he always said to those who
went to confession to him:

When I go to hear confessions—I still can't, because
to go out to hear confessions . . . from here it's impossible to go out, but that's another problem—when
I used to go to hear confessions in my previous diocese, people would come to me and I would always
ask them: "Do you give alms?" "Yes, Father!" "Very
good." And I would ask them two further questions:
"Tell me, when you give alms, do you look the person
in the eye?" "Oh I don't know, I haven't really thought
about it." The second question: "And when you give
alms, do you touch the hand of the person you are giv-
ing them to or do you toss the coin at him or her?" This
is the problem: the flesh of Christ, touching the flesh
of Christ, taking upon ourselves this suffering for the
poor.

It is not enough, therefore, to give alms, Bergoglio explained; it is necessary to look the poor person in the eye
and to touch his hand. Because in that way one touches
"the flesh of Christ". The Pope continued:

Poverty for us Christians is not a sociological, philo-
sophical, or cultural category, no. It is theological. I
might say this is the first category, because our God,
the Son of God, abased himself, he made himself poor

to walk along the road with us. This is our poverty: the poverty of the flesh of Christ, the poverty that brought the Son of God to us through his Incarnation. A poor Church for the poor begins by reaching out to the flesh of Christ. If we reach out to the flesh of Christ, we begin to understand something, to understand what this poverty, the Lord's poverty, actually is.

"Open the empty convents for the refugees"

We pray for a heart which will embrace immigrants.
God will judge us upon how we have treated the
most needy.

@Pontifex (on Twitter), July 8, 2013

I n the first six months of his pontificate, Pope Francis
decided twice to manifest concretely his closeness to
immigrants and refugees. In July he made his first visit
outside of Rome to Lampedusa, the island outpost of
Italy which is the destination of the old, unsafe boats that
bring unfortunate people seeking a better life. Later, on
Tuesday, September 10, he traveled to pay a private visit,
far from the television cameras, to the refugees of the
Astalli Center of the Jesuits which, in the heart of Rome,
a few steps from the *Piazza Venezia*, for more than thirty
years has welcomed, fed, and helped persons who have
arrived in Italy while fleeing from wars, violence, and torture. From there he sent an unmistakable message, which
surely has caused more than one person to jump up from
his chair: "Empty convents are not to be sold to be transformed into hotels to make money for the Church", but
rather are to be used by refugees.

For the Pope who dreams of "a poor Church for the poor", being truly close to those who suffer is not a talking-point for some homily, but rather a program for his pontificate that requires daily witness. Francis arrived in a modest Ford Focus, without any escort, without entourage, and without a secretary. He greeted many of those who were waiting, as they do every day, so as to be able to eat a meal on the premises of the Center. Then he entered and went downstairs to the basement dining room, approaching the guests who were eating there; then he lingered with about twenty refugees. He listened to their terrifying stories, including a particularly moving one by the Syrian woman Carol, who told the Pope: "Our boys were all enlisted or killed in a war that to us was senseless. . . ."

After greeting all the staff and sipping a bit of maté, the typical herbal beverage of South America, Francis went to the nearby Church of the Gesù, where he met other victims of wars and the volunteers who serve in four shelters run by the Jesuit Service for Refugees. And he spoke, looking up several times from his prepared speech:

> Many of you are Muslims or of other religions; you come from many countries and from different situations. We must not be afraid of differences! Brotherhood allows us to discover that diversity is wealth, a gift for all! . . .
>
> [Rome should be] a city that allows them to rediscover the human dimension, to begin to smile again. However, how often here, as in other places, are many people whose stay permits bear the words "interna-

tional protection" forced to live in impoverished or at times degrading conditions, without the chance to begin a dignified life, to plan a new future?

The Pope explained that "Serving means to welcome with care persons as they arrive, to reach out to them, without calculation and without fear, with tenderness and understanding, just as Jesus bent down to wash the feet of the apostles. . . ." Francis added that the word "solidarity" "frightens the more developed world. They try not to say it. It is almost a bad word for them. But it is our word!" Francis continued:

> The poor are also the preferential teachers of our knowledge of God; their frailty and simplicity unmask our selfishness, our false security, our pretense of self-sufficiency, and they guide us to the experience of God's closeness and tenderness, to receive his love into our life, his mercy as the Father who, discreetly and with patient confidence, takes care of us all.

Bergoglio went on to explain:

> To welcome is not enough. It is not enough to offer a sandwich if this is not accompanied by the possibility of learning to stand on one's own two feet. Charity that leaves the poor in the same situation as before is not adequate. True mercy, the kind that God gives and teaches us, requires justice, requires that the poor find the way out of their poverty. . . .
> For the whole Church it is important that receiving the poor and promoting justice should not simply be entrusted to "specialists", but rather should be

the focus of all pastoral care, of the formation of future priests and religious, of the normal duties of all parishes, ecclesial movements, and groups.

Then came the invitation not to leave church buildings empty. "In particular—this is important, I say it from the heart—I would like to invite religious Institutes to read this sign of the times seriously and with a sense of responsibility. The Lord is calling us to experience more courageously and generously this welcoming of the needy into our communities, our houses, our empty convents."

"Dear consecrated religious," he said, growing more eloquent, "Empty convents are not to be sold to be transformed into hotels to make money for the Church. The empty convents are not ours, they are for the flesh of Christ, for the refugees. The Lord is calling us to welcome them generously and courageously in the empty convents." Certainly, the Pope added, this is not a simple task; "it requires of us discernment, responsibility, but also courage. We do much, but perhaps we are called to do more."

Francis concluded:

[We are called] to overcome the temptation of spiritual worldliness so as to be close to simple persons and above all to the least. We need communities of solidarity that live out love in a concrete way! Every day, here and in other centers, many persons, most of them young, get in line for a hot meal. These persons remind us of the sufferings and tragedies of humanity. But this line also tells us that it is possible, now, for everyone to do something.

To Pray "with the flesh"

The globalization of indifference has taken from us the ability to weep!

Homily in Lampedusa, July 8, 2013

I t is necessary to pray "with the flesh". The Pope said this during the homily of his morning Mass at the Domus Sanctae Marthae on June 5, 2013. Speaking about persons who live "in the subsoil of existence", in "dire" conditions, and who have lost hope, and commenting on the readings of the day which spoke about the experiences of Tobit and Sarah, the Pope said: "They do not curse but they complain. . . . Lamenting to God is not a sin."

Bergoglio then related this incident: "A priest I know once said to a woman who complained to God about her misfortunes: 'Madam, that is a kind of prayer, go ahead. The Lord feels and hears our lamentations.'" Expressing sorrow, Francis explained, "is human", also because "there are many people who are in these situations of existential suffering."

The Pope then spoke about the Gospel passage from Mark, which tells about the Sadducees who question Jesus about the widow of the seven brothers. The Sadducees, the Pontiff said, presented her as though "in a laboratory, quite aseptic, a moral case". Instead, "when we speak about these people who are in these extreme situations", we must do so "with our hearts close to them". We must think "about these people, whose suffering is so great, with our heart and with our flesh". And he said that he does not appreciate it "when people talk about these situations in an academic, inhuman way", perhaps merely citing statistics.

"In the Church there are many people in this situation", and if someone asks what should be done, the Pontiff's reply is: "what Jesus says: we must pray, pray for them." These suffering people, the Pope added, "must enter my heart, they must be an anxiety for me. My brother is suffering, my sister is suffering; this is the mystery of the communion of saints. Pray: Lord, look at him who cries and suffers. Let us pray, if I may say so, with our flesh." We should pray with our flesh, then, and "not with ideas; pray with your heart", he repeated.

∽

The Multiplication of the "Empanadas"

Never tire of working for a more just world, marked by greater solidarity!

Address to the Community of Varginha,
Rio de Janeiro, July 25, 2013

On May 30, 2013, the Pope celebrated in the Basilica of St. John Lateran his first Mass on the Feast of Corpus Christi.

In his homily he meditated on the Gospel incident of the multiplication of the loaves and fishes described by Luke the Evangelist.

Francis underscored Jesus' invitation to his disciples when faced with the hungry crowd: "You give them something to eat." The Pope wondered:

What does Jesus' request to the disciples, that they themselves give food to the multitude, come from? It comes from two things: first of all from the crowd, who in following Jesus find themselves in the open air, far from any inhabited areas, while evening is falling; and then from the concern of the disciples who ask Jesus to send

the crowd away so that they can go to the neighbor-
ing villages to find provisions and somewhere to stay.
Faced with the needs of the crowd the disciples' solution was this: let each one think of himself—send the
crowd away! How often do we Christians have this
temptation! We do not take upon ourselves the needs
of others, but dismiss them with a pious: "God help
you", or with a not so pious "good luck", and if I never
see you again. . . .

Jesus' solution goes in another direction, which surprises the disciples: "You give them something to eat."
But the disciples answer that they have only five loaves
and two fish. "Jesus is not discouraged", the Pope said.

> [He] asks the disciples to have the people sit down in
> groups of fifty people. He looks up to heaven, recites
> the blessing, breaks the bread and fish into pieces and
> gives them to the disciples to distribute. It is a moment
> of deep *communion*: the crowd is satisfied by the word
> of the Lord and is now nourished by his bread of life.
> And they were all satisfied, the Evangelist notes.

The miracle of multiplication comes about, in part,
through sharing. In the book *Francisco: El Papa de la gente*
[Francis: The people's Pope], published in Spanish by
Aguilar, the journalist Evangelina Himitian related an incident that concerns Bergoglio. "I can say", the author
recounts, "that once I saw him multiply food, as Jesus
did with the loaves and fishes."

It was October 2012 and the journalist was collabo-
rating with the press office of the Catholic-Evangelical
ecumenical meetings; Cardinal Bergoglio was one of the

organizers. "In the stadium where the meeting was being held," Evangelina Himitian explains,

> the management did not allow anyone to bring in food, and therefore during the breaks everyone present had to buy something to eat instead. There was not much of a choice: all they had were *empanadas*, the typical meat-filled pastries; moreover they were scarce. It was a national holiday and there were no other events on the program. Someone asked Bergoglio whether he would rather go dine in the exclusive Puerto Madero district, a short walk from the stadium, in which there were several elegant restaurants, but he replied that he would remain to eat with all the others.

"When we journalists took a break for dinner," Evangelina goes on to relate in the epilogue of her book, "it was already very late and practically nothing was left."

> While we were walking through the room where the food was served, Bergoglio walked up to us, greeted us one by one and thanked us for our work. We sat down at the last table. The waitress brought us a plate with five *empanadas*, but there were eight of us. Someone took the initiative and began to cut them in half. Sharing: that was the spirit of the meeting. Anyway, we had no other choice.
>
> From his table at the other end of the room Bergoglio saw what we were doing and understood. He got up and began to ask the other customers whether they had finished eating. He gathered from the hands of the pastors and priests the last *empanadas*, arranged them on a plate and brought them to us. Moved by his attentive

gesture, we felt flattered and quite astonished. He had multiplied the food. That little miracle of his remained etched on our hearts. The man who today occupies the See of Peter had seen a need and had filled it, whereas nobody else had noticed it.

～

From Prison to the Pope's Altar:
Gabriela's Hosts

I ask you to be builders of the world, to work for a better world. Dear young people, please, don't be observers of life, . . . but immerse yourself in the reality of life, as Jesus did.

Address to Young People,
Waterfront of Copacabana, July 27, 2013

From the first days of his pontificate, Pope Francis has tried to show in concrete ways that he is close to the imprisoned. This concern is in keeping with that of his predecessors, from John XXIII—who paid a visit to the prisoners of Regina Coeli a few weeks after his election —down to Benedict XVI, whose dialogue with the prisoners of Rebibbia should be remembered as one of the most beautiful and moving pages of his pontificate. It is well known that Francis decided to celebrate the Mass of the Lord's Supper, on Holy Thursday, in the juvenile detention center *Casal del Marmo*, and on several occasions he has cited—on Twitter also—the passage from the Gospel of Matthew (chapter 25) in which Jesus declares that anything done for the poor, the suffering, the hungry and thirsty, or the imprisoned will be as though it had been done for him personally.

From Argentina comes the story of another female prisoner in contact with Pope Francis. She is Gabriela Caballero, who is thirty-eight years old and prepared the hosts used by the Pontiff for his Mass at the Domus Sanctae Marthae. Gabriela has been detained since 2010 in unit 47 of San Martín Penitentiary near Buenos Aires, and must serve a seven-year prison term. Francis learned about her and her workshop for making communion wafers during breakfast on July 16, 2013, from the Ordinary of San Isidro, Bishop Oscar Vicente Ojea. The prelate tells the story: "I delivered to the Pope the letter and the photographs of the workshop that Gabriela had sent him. The Pope was very impressed that this young woman made the hosts with which he celebrates Mass." Francis, the bishop also said, "took the packet without opening it and personally brought it to his apartment."

On July 17 the Pope wrote in his own hand a short letter thanking the detained woman, and on July 18 he celebrated the first Mass with some of these hosts.

Dear Gabriela,

Bishop Ojea brought me your letter. Thank you for your confidence and also for the hosts. Starting tomorrow I will celebrate Mass with these hosts, and I can assure you that it is something that moves me. Your letter made me reflect and therefore I will pray for you. It gladdens me and assures me to know that you are praying for me too. You will be close to me. Thanks again for having written to me and for the photographs: I will keep them in front of me on my desk. May Jesus bless you and may the Blessed Virgin take care of you.

—Francis

Bishop Ojea remarks: "What impressed me most about the Pope's letter is the sentence in which he says that he is assured by the fact that she is praying for him. It struck me that the Holy Father feels secure thanks to a person who is insecure because she is deprived of her freedom. This is almost a paradox: to be assured by the prayer of a person who is suffering."

Gabriela granted an interview, with her "guardian angel" at her side, the prison chaplain, Fr. Jorge Garcia Cuerva, and recalled that the priest was the one to inform her by telephone that the Pope had responded with a personal letter. "I know Bishop Ojea," the woman said, "since he often comes to visit us. When I heard that he was going to see the Pope, I had no doubt at all: this was the chance to give the Pope some of our artisanal hosts and some photographs of our workshop."

"Honestly," she added, "I did not imagine that he would reply. I did not want to kid myself. . . . My associates told me: the Pope will write to you. He answers all letters. This Pope wants to reach everyone and everywhere. He wants to be close to the people, and we are people.

"It made me happy to learn that the Pope's letter was a reply just to me. To read 'Dear Gabriela' struck me, since I am deprived of freedom and in a place with so many dark hours. I am happy to know that from a prison it is possible to reach the Vatican."